Frommer's®

Born to Shop

CARIBBEAN
PORTS OF CALL
1st EDITION

THE ULTIMATE GUIDE FOR
TRAVELERS WHO LOVE TO SHOP

Suzy Gershman

Suzy Gershman

BORN TO SHOP

CARIBBEAN PORTS OF CALL

The Ultimate Guide for
Travelers Who Love to Shop

1st Edition

MACMILLAN • USA

For my father, who taught me how to dance.

MACMILLAN TRAVEL
A Simon & Schuster Macmillan Company
1633 Broadway
New York, NY 10019

Find us online at **http://www.mgr.com/travel** or on America
Online at Keyword: **Frommer's.**

ISBN 0-02860712-0
ISSN 1093-3204

Editor: Kelly Regan
Production Editor: Carol Sheehan
Design by George McKeon
Digital Cartography by Raffaele DeGennaro

CONTENTS

MAP LIST

WHAT THE SYMBOL MEANS

· ·

 SUZY'S FAVORITES
Stores, restaurants, and accommodations you
should not miss.

TO START WITH

The book you have in your hands actually began when I was 11 years old and relates to the path that led me to become The Shopping Lady. At the time, my father had been transferred to Caracas, Venezuela, for six months. So, we all moved down to live in an apartment in Las Mercedes, and I busied myself by flirting with the *fruitero's* son.

On the way home we stopped off at several Caribbean Islands. In Haiti, my father gave me 50¢ and said, "Here, see what you can buy with this."

My career was begun.

(I bought a wooden sculpture, thank you very much.)

While Haiti is not included in these pages, I have returned to the Caribbean a number of times since that fateful trip. Nowadays, I usually go by cruise ship, to take in as many ports as possible. This edition is primarily aimed at cruise passengers who are sailing to the big shopping islands, but there's quite enough to be of use to the beach-and-honeymoon set as well.

I've traveled on just about every major cruise line to research this book. The cover was shot by Ian Cook on board the *QE2*, which only sails to the Caribbean for a limited time each year. I send thanks to everyone on board all the ships who helped with the photography and the research. Special thanks to Mary Jo McNally, who braved hurricane season with me to do some of the work.

Anchors aweigh to all . . .

Chapter One

· · · · · · · ·

THE BEST OF THE CARIBBEAN

CARIBBEAN ABUNDANCE

· ·

It's difficult to compile a meaningful best of list to any destination, let alone one as diverse as the Caribbean. It's difficult to island-hop unless you fly your own plane, and the best bets and best buys very much depend on the size of your wallet and the very reasons you chose the Caribbean. If you came for the isolation, to chill out, to honeymoon, or to escape the real world, then shopping is going to be low on your list of priorities anyway, and you certainly won't (and shouldn't) go out of your way to track down one or two addresses dotted here and there.

I've tried to gear this list toward the mainstream islands that most cruise ships visit, so it will be of use to most people. Any store chosen in these pages is written about later in the book, but this can serve as a short list of must-do's, if you can match your island choices to this group.

In some cases, I have provided two answers to a category because I believe there are two Caribbeans—the rich, isolated, hidden, private, and personal Caribbean where royalty and rich folks tuck away from the winter winds; and the real world Caribbean, seen on the surface as offered up to cruise ship passengers, day-trippers, and those who will not go off the beaten path.

I must also say that when asked what is the best of the Caribbean, I have to vote for emotional experiences rather than specific stores or islands—nothing beats a drive through tropical countryside, a gourmet lunch of Caribbean cuisine, a luxury hideaway with a beach, and just a few really good stores. *That* is the best of the Caribbean, in a coconut shell.

THE BEST ISLAND FOR A 1-DAY SHOPPING SPREE

Rich Man: St. Barts

St. Barts is hard to get to and local retailers do not want cruise ships in port, making this exactly the sort of country club that Groucho Marx identified by saying, "I wouldn't want to be a member of any club that would have me." The really good ones simply don't want outsiders. That understood, St. Barts is a French island not far from St. Martin/St. Maarten that is served by Cunard's *Sea Goddess,* some private yachts, and a bigger ship or two every now and then. Prices are outrageously expensive, but you cannot deny the chic that permeates the air. If money is no object, this is your place.

Poor Man: Antigua

Talk about the Comeback Kid: Antigua reinvented itself after hurricane damage and offers a sensational combination of pleasures. The ships dock right downtown, a few meters from the stores. The stores are bright, clean, new, and laid out in walking distance; and while there is a shopping center, there is no "mall" atmosphere. You are encouraged to stroll and shop and poke around a little. Several excellent shops sell real clothes for real people, not crazy resort items you wouldn't be caught dead in once you sober up. If you need to chill in high luxury, check out Jumby Bay.

THE BEST ON-BOARD SHOPPING

Most cruise ships are dedicated to the concept of shopping on board. Why not? There's a lot of revenue to be made. The newer the ship, the more likely it is to have several well-stocked, even creative, stores and to pride itself on its ability to match prices on land.

Especially unique lines that offer the best of buying and browsing:

- Celebrity, with several new megaships that have not only regular stores but showrooms where you can borrow products to test them—such as the Sony Showroom;
- Costa, the European division of Carnival with on-board malls created specifically for European shoppers;
- Disney—shopping is not Mickey Mouse to these guys.

THE BEST REAL PEOPLE BARGAIN SHOPPING

MARSHALL'S
Old San Juan, Puerto Rico.

If you realize you need basics like underwear, panty hose (you're kidding?), a bathing suit, or any of those things that are important to the trip but on which you don't want to spend a fortune or even pay resort retail, head to Marshall's, one of America's top off-pricers. This isn't the best Marshall's you've ever been to, but they can probably solve the problem for a lot less than it would cost you on board.

THE BEST SHOPPING AD CAMPAIGN

LITTLE SWITZERLAND
Little Switzerland is a chain of luxury shops selling a little of everything; they have stores not only all

over the Caribbean but even in Alaska. Since there are (at last count) 10 stores on different Caribbean islands, you should have no trouble finding one. Whether you shop there or not, you have to congratulate them on wonderful ads that appear in most travel- and cruise-related consumer magazines. Most of their ads are well done, but this prize goes to the ad that pictures a cruise ship in the distance and a long row of women marching through the seas from ship to shore. The headline: "Women and Credit Cards First."

Second place goes to Jeweler's Warehouse for an ad that pictures a lime green T-shirt in the center of a white page. Printed on the T-shirt is this slogan: "My daughter went to the Virgin Islands and all I got was a 14k gold ring with a faceted oval sapphire surrounded by 16 round brilliant-cut diamonds."

THE BEST SHOPPER'S CONVENIENCE GIMMICK

Royal Caribbean International has a series of private Crown & Anchor Clubs dotted in assorted turnaround cities all over the world. To serve the Caribbean, there are clubs in St. Thomas and San Juan.

The idea is that passengers who have time between getting on and off their ship and getting on and off their airplane have some downtime in which they are loaded down with luggage and carry-ons. During which they'd love to shop, have a place to sit down, use the rest rooms, maybe have a drink, and just be comfortable. Like an airline lounge or club.

The Crown & Anchor Club in Charlotte Amalie is 3,300 square feet, located in Hibiscus Alley in the midst of the local shopping heartbeat. The Crown & Anchor Club in San Juan is located at 257 Calle Justo, just off Calle Fortaleza in Old San Juan and also right in the shopping district.

Passengers may check their shopping bags at the club during their spree, dart in and out of the lounge to freshen up, have a drink or light snack, and then go back to continue their shopping spree.

Royal Caribbean says their San Juan passengers spend approximately $4 million a year shopping in San Juan before or after boarding a San Juan based RCCL ship. Good goin', guys.

THE BEST ITINERARY FOR SHOPPERS

Some cruise lines call this the Southern Caribbean, others call it Eastern Caribbean—if you want to shop 'til you drop, look for a ship that starts off in San Juan and gives you Martinique, Barbados, Antigua, St. Martin / St. Maarten, and St. Thomas.

One of the newer trends in cruising is the 4-day cruise. Check out either the 4-day Cunard *Sea Goddess* cruise that gives you lots of St. Thomas and then St. Barts, or perhaps the 4-day that gives you San Juan, St. Thomas, and St. Martin / St. Maarten. If you have the kids along and can't do too much shopping, but want to pack in a wallop for each member of the family, the Disney combination does give you plenty of Disney magic (sorry) and a day in duty-free Nassau, Bahamas.

THE BEST BET FOR WESTERN CARIBBEAN SHOPPERS

Los Cinco Soles
Cozumel, Mexico.

Cozumel will certainly be your best shopping day on a Western Caribbean tour; this store is a bit far down the *malecón* (sea road), but it's worth the walk. They sell everything except fake French perfumes and have a place where you can get a drink or snack as well.

THE BEST SHOPPING SURPRISE

French pharmacies in Martinique carry all your favorite brands of beauty products that can't be found in the United States, including Galenic (my favorite), Vichy, Orangerine, and others.

THE BEST KITSCH

This is hard, because let me tell you, Caribbean kitsch is almost an oxymoron. But nonetheless, if I only have one vote here, I give it to the ballpoint pen I found on board *Monarch of the Seas*. It had a tiny plastic replica of the ship, complete with island and palm trees, stuck out on a plastic limb so that when you write, the ship and the island and the palm trees all move around in a circle. About $4.

THE BEST BATIK

JAVA WRAPS
Christiansted, St. Croix.

Hurricane damage sent this firm back to their home in St. Croix to rebuild—which makes it harder to find their wonderful designs. Java Wraps uses the Dutch wax method of batik but does it in a modern enough manner that their clothing is colorful, exciting, and wearable—anywhere.

THE BEST POSTCARDS

NEWS CAFÉ
South Beach, Miami, Florida.

Not just any postcards mind you, but the ones that are artistic renditions of the famed art deco hotels. They are $1 each, which I admit is high, but they so capture the spirit of South Beach and everything that light and architecture and fun and sun stand for; they are absolutely the best in the biz.

THE CUTEST STOREFRONT

Maison Creole tries to be cute in their downtown Fort-de-France store, but their quayside shop in Martinique is adorable—photo ops galore.

THE BEST FOODSTUFFS

I'm a big one in bringing back local foodstuffs as gifts; just make sure that you pack anything liquid, runny, or gooey in a plastic bag. These are my faves for munching and bringing home to loved ones; some of these items have distribution on several islands.

- Suzy's Hot Sauce, Antigua;
- Spicy Caribbee plantains, Old San Juan;
- Spicy Caribbee spice packets, Old San Juan;
- Mexican vanilla, Cozumel;
- A really great bottle of rum, such as Mount Gay (from Barbados) or Bacardi (from Puerto Rico). See entry for "rum" in Chapter 5's "Dictionary of Caribbean Life & Style" for a more detailed explanation of the region's rums.

THE BEST GIFTS UNDER $10

Foodstuffs do make great gifts and usually cost less than $10, but here are some other choices:

- Sunny Caribbee soaps, sold in colorful cotton baggies, bright colors (bags and soaps), and Caribbean flavors (bran, carrot, etc.), $4–$5 per unit;
- Pusser's tin cup, not for golfers but for drinking out of. It's ideal for travel, it won't break, it's white tin with etchings of old sailing ships, and it costs about $10;

- Barbados reversible rag doll, $7;
- Logo merchandise from your ship.

THE BEST PERFUME SHOP

· ·

ROGER ALBERT
Fort-de-France, Martinique.

A good perfume shop has a few basic requirements: It must be located on a French island, and it must have a business base of local and visiting French, not tourists. This guarantees that the local reputation is intact and that the marketplace is plugged in to the needs of the most sophisticated shoppers, since cruise passengers are more easily fooled than residents.

Beyond this, you have the issue of selection. Many perfume shops in the Caribbean are aligned with only certain fragrance houses or distributors—they can't get every brand. This is why you go from door to door, asking for your preferred fragrance. Only Roger Albert, of all shops in the Basin, carries every single brand, including many esoteric ones you may have never heard of.

You get a 20% discount; they will do mail order to the U.S. and Europe.

THE BEST LEGAL FAKES

· ·

GUCCI
Assorted Islands.

If I knew the strict technicalities of this, believe me, I'd tell you. All I know is that when I took the Gucci bag I bought in the Caribbean to Gucci in New York to be repaired, they died laughing and said they only repaired real Gucci. I showed the receipt, the whole bit. They said Gucci in the Caribbean is a franchise operation. Someone else told me that through a legal loophole, the people that run these Gucci shops have the rights to use the Gucci name, and that some of their goods are outright fakes and some are Gray market, brought in from Asia.

I did buy a big black handbag on a recent visit; it was stunning and well priced at $168. That's not cheap, but it seemed fair. I received the bag in a felt protective bag, in tissue, and then in a Gucci shopping bag. I was proud of myself until I noticed on the bottom of the shopping bag the words "Made in El Salvador." Tell me, do you think the real Italian Gucci has bags made in El Salvador?

THE BEST LEGAL / ILLEGAL SHOPPING EXPERIENCE

Smoking a Cuban cigar (Havana) outside the U.S. OK, so the law is that you have to embargo Cuban-made goods in the U.S., but when you are in the Caribbean Basin, in foreign countries, you can legally buy and enjoy a Havana or two dozen. The term "Havana" has come to mean cigar made in Havana in order to distiniguish it from a cigar made elsewhere, possibly even by the same firm that still exists in Havana. Anyway, let's remember our fifth grade civics lessons: Puerto Rico and the U.S. Virgin Islands are a part of the U.S., so anyone claiming to sell "real" Havanas there is lying or cheating you or performing an illegal act.

So, light up already.

THE WORST ILLEGAL SHOPPING EXPERIENCE

Getting busted trying to enter the U.S. with Cuban cigars.

THE BEST MULTIPLE OR CHAIN STORE

BODY SHOP
St. John's, Antigua.

Yes, it at first begins like a regular branch of any of the hundreds of Body Shops around the world, but in the back, the merchandise selection fans into local arts and crafts that provide a double whammy. Not only is the selection stylish and fun, but it segues from Anita Rodnick's Save the Rainforest philosophy and gives the store more depth. Brilliant.

THE BEST SUNGLASSES

Rich Man: You can often find big name European designer sunglasses at great prices in the bins of discontinued styles at any of the many general stores that dot the Caribbean. I got a pair of Christian Lacroix sunglasses—far too chic for anyone save Holly Golightly—for $20, marked down from $180 at Ashland's in St. Maarten.

Poor Man: Hmmmm, as much as I hate to see Sunglass Huts moving into every available storefront in Florida—I actually cringe when I see a Sunglass Hut anywhere—the truth is that they have good prices, a large selection, and are often the smartest choice if you need a pair of shades. They aren't really discounted, but they carry the lot ends of the major names such as Ray Bans. So you get an excellent price on Ray Bans, which is among the best brands when it comes to sun safety, which has to be an issue here, long before fashion and style.

THE BEST FACTORY OUTLET

Note that Belz is opening a brand new factory outlet mall in San Juan in the end of 1998 so this could impact the entire category. For now, let's go for:

- Mount Gay Rum Factory, Barbados
- Ralph Lauren / Polo Factory Store, Old San Juan

THE BEST SPECIALTY SHOPPING EVENT

. . . .

ANNUAL ANTIQUES FLEA MARKET
Whim Plantation, St. Croix.

It's usually held in March. Yes, dealers fly in for it.

THE BEST CIGAR SHOP

. . . .

LA CASA DEL HABANO
St. John's, Antigua.

La Casa del Habano is a chain or a franchise or something, but I like this one because I got into a chat with the managing director and he was terrific. Also, the store has a huge selection, gives away free matches (great souvenir), and guarantees the product—important in a land where counterfeits abound.

THE BEST MAINSTREAM CARIBBEAN DESIGNER

. . . .

BASE
Antigua.

This Antigua-based design team has a few shops in the Caribbean and is moving Stateside. They sort of do a Calvin Klein–Giorgio Armani simple thing with a teenage edge. It's certainly not what you expect from a Caribbean island and is very wearable, any place in the world. Lots of beige, white, and black, in solids, of course.

THE BEST HOTEL GIFT SHOP

. . . .

GATSBY'S
Sandy Lane, Barbados.

Gatsby's actually has several boutiques dotted around the island, even one at the cruise ship terminal. But the fanciest is, of course, inside the Sandy Lane hotel where big name designer sunglasses, sandals, straw hats, and sundresses are sold alongside proper dinner clothes for those who know that the "veddy, veddy" still dress for dinner in Barbados.

THE BEST PIER SHOPPING, FIRST PLACE

DEEPWATER PIER
Barbados.

A cruise terminal mall with one of every major store joined with an information center, a driveway for taxis, and an additional chattel-house TT (tourist trap) center with more fun and color than you'll find just about anywhere else in the Caribbean. Great place to buy Upside Down Rag Dolls. (Look under the skirt of the doll—voilà—another head, flip her skirt and she's reversible.)

THE BEST PIER SHOPPING, SECOND PLACE

HAVENSIGHT MALL
St. Thomas.

Convenient and pleasant but without the energy you find at Deepwater Pier in Barbados. This is simply a series of strip malls laid out sort of California style, with a branch of most big stores, and you can buy everything from foods and snack items to Gucci handbags.

THE BEST AIRPORT SHOPPING

MIAMI INTERNATIONAL AIRPORT
They sell it all here.

THE BEST SNACK & SHOP
. . . .

LE SELECT
Gustavia, St. Barts.

What can I tell you, there isn't a piece of Caribbean literature that doesn't rave about the cheeseburgers here, or fail to note that Mick Jagger loves 'em.

Chapter Two

· · · · · · · ·

CARIBBEAN DETAILS

WELCOME TO THE CARIBBEAN

· ·

I live in a place where the leaves fall off the trees in November, where snow falls all winter, and where the brightest color you will see for months on end is that of flames dancing in the fireplace. I live in a place where every time we have a blizzard, my husband yells at me—as if it was my fault. I live in a place where the winter light is gray and mean and can depress even the most jolly souls.

The Caribbean was invented for folks like me who live in places like this: The quality of sunlight alone is worth spending several hours on a plane. Stepping into a store where the walls are painted turquoise and the stereo is blaring hot music, a bang, bang beat with words that seem to suggest I need "somebody to jam you tonight" is worth it all.

The light and the weather, the palm trees and the color all go down fine. The silliness and the sassiness—yeah, sign me up. After all these things, *then* I can think about shopping in the Caribbean.

The shopping in the Caribbean, on the whole, isn't the best in the world. But there are some secret good buys to be found and some rather astounding savings on certain items. So don't give up on me now.

I confess, I don't go to the Caribbean just to go shopping. And I confess that just about every time

I'm about to launch into a speech about how careful you have to be not to get cheated in the Caribbean, that's when I find another bargain worth bragging about. I admit that when I am feeling jaded and over-shopped and preachy and passé, well, that's when I find the secret buy that simply makes the whole trip.

Furthermore, of all the places in the world except maybe Hong Kong and Istanbul, I can't think of a region more laden with shopping potholes and pitfalls. I don't care what sort of shopping pro you think you are, you need my help here. Let's face it, there's good shopping in the Caribbean and cheat shopping in the Caribbean, with a lot of tricks going down.

There are still good buys here; you have to get lucky with some of them, and you have to know how to find the others. There's a whole lot to learn, even if you aren't a serious shopper—*especially* if you're not a serious shopper. You also have to stay sober long enough to make a smart purchase or two!

Everyone will do some shopping, whether on a cruise, a one-island visit, or even a honeymoon. So we might as well follow in the footsteps of the great Sy Syms, who has always claimed, "an educated shopper is my best customer."

I go to the Caribbean not to buy one thing or to visit one destination but for the whole of it, and invariably, I go on a cruise ship. One year we tried a week on our favorite island and hated it: in-season high prices, tons of tourists, bad (and expensive) food—in other words, rip-off city. I left angry and desperate to get to London—yes, winter in London. I don't even like that Caribbean island any more!

Now, I usually visit the islands via one of the many cruise ships that take to the seas. There's something for everyone on a cruise ship, and the idea of a new day in a new port is something that appeals to my wanderlust. When I seek variety, I pick a different type of ship or a different route, but I find

The Caribbean Islands

FLORIDA

Miami

Straits of Florida

THE BAHAMAS

Havana

Cuba

Little Cayman

Grand Cayman   Cayman Brac

CAYMAN ISLANDS

Montego Bay

JAMAICA

Kingston

Haiti

Port-au-Prince

GREATER

C a r i b b e a n   S e a

COLOMBIA

2-0231

0 [scale bar] 250 mi
402 km
N

Atlantic   Ocean

TURKS AND CAICOS ISLANDS

VIRGIN   ISLANDS

St. Thomas
Tortola
Anegada
San Juan
Virgin Gorda
Anguilla
St. Maarten/
St. Martin
Barbuda

Dominican Republic

Santo
Domingo

Puerto Rico

St. John
Saba

St. Croix

St. Kitts
Antigua

St. Barthélemy

Nevis
Montserrat

ANTILLES

St. Eustatius

Guadeloupe

Dominica

Martinique

St. Lucia

St. Vincent

Barbados

DUTCH LEEWARD ISLANDS

THE
GRENADINES

Aruba   Curaçao

Bonaire

LESSER ANTILLES

Grenada

LEEWARD ISLANDS

WINDWARD ISLANDS

Tobago

Port of Spain

Trinidad

Caracas

VENEZUELA

GUYANA

comfort and protection in the fact that when I tour with a cruise, I am taken care of in a manner that I may not be able to arrange when I'm on my own.

This book is a bit different from the others in the series because there are so many different places within its pages; it was really written for the cruise passenger who will visit several places and doesn't know where to shop and when to hold off. If you're bound for just one or two islands, I hope I can help out. If you're on a cruise, I know you need this book.

So welcome to almost perpetual sunshine, never-ending rum cocktails, people who do the Macarena while they shop, and the beat of the calypso band. Welcome to deals and steals, welcome to scams and fakes and designer cheats, welcome to good times, many hellos, and several good buys.

CARIBBEAN FANTASIES

During the winter of our discontent, it's easy to think of the Caribbean—especially if you live in the snowy states of the Northeast or Midwest. I make it through Christmas rather joyfully, but come mid-January, begin to dream of another clime. It's not hard. Newspapers and billboards beckon us to sunshine and palm trees; cruise ships have more berths than ever to fill and offer more affordable means of escape than ever before.

As the snowdrifts pile up, we collect our free brochures, look at the ads closely, and begin to think seriously of how to escape the winter blahs. And because we know a good deal when we see one, we begin to dream Caribbean dreams.

Many people fantasize about deserted beaches, coral sands, frothy cocktails, and limitless tennis. They dream of scuba diving among neon fish, of clear, clean water the color of turquoise, of rooms without telephones, and shopping without taxes.

What's so wonderful about the Caribbean is that many of these fantasies can come true. But the Caribbean is a vast area, with five distinct geographic designations, and each island has its own personality. Often, Caribbean fantasies can't match Caribbean realities, and I've seen more rip-offs than I care to tell about.

So I warn you now in a way that your travel agent won't. If your idea of the perfect vacation is to shop till you drop—go to Paris. Or London. Or the Mall of America. If you're looking for picture-book charm of the cobbled-street, window-boxed, and geranium-filled kind, try Provence, or the Cotswold. Give Lisbon a whirl.

The Caribbean is the Caribbean. It's near, it's affordable, it can be unrelentingly gorgeous—from the right vantage point. Give me a week in St. Barts and a $20,000 shopping allowance, with a bungalow overlooking the sea and unlimited French francs to pay for gourmet meals and burgers, and sure, that's a nice trip to incorporate into anyone's lifestyle. But aside from a dream vacation like that, there is a real world to deal with in the Caribbean.

In the real world, every shop on every island put together couldn't hold their own in Paris or Milan; there is much tourist junk and clutter, and often international mobs of people (tourists all) will be perusing the shops in search of the same bargains as you. Everybody wants the $99 diamonds. Everybody wants the cutie pie magnets, the Cuban cigars, the tie-dyed T-shirts.

So here it is up front: *Don't let your fantasies of shopping the Caribbean ruin your trip.*

Sportspeople and active types will adore the Caribbean; beach bunnies and kids will adore the Caribbean; overstressed types who care for no more than a beach chair and a tall, cool drink will love the Caribbean. But shopoholics? Well, browse-and-tell shoppers can have a ball. But serious, heavy-duty, big-time, big-gun, designer gung-ho types may be disappointed . . . or just merely limited. On the other hand, if you wanted an Hermès tie for $106, instead of the $135 they charge at Hermès in New York, you've come to the right place after all.

It's a matter of facing up to reality and not dreaming too big of a shopping dream.

YOUR CARIBBEAN SHOPPING CART

Before your dream of that great duty free in the sky, remember that Caribbean ports are great for certain types of merchandise and downright crummy for others. There are exceptions to these rules, but generally speaking you won't be disappointed with price or selection if you're thinking about buying:

Crystal   Crystal bargains abound on all types of international big names, mostly French and English. Prices are standard throughout the islands and are approximately 25% less than in the United States; prices are almost identical to those in Europe. The big trick here is to be able to carry your purchases with you; once you get into shipping you will wipe out most of your savings. Also note that the amount of the savings varies with the brands, not the island. You'll save more on Orrefors than on Bacarrat (although I have seen some awfully good Bacarrat prices!). In fact, Orrefors in the Caribbean is less expensive than in Sweden, where it's made!

China   The best news for china shoppers is that some stores stock odd pieces and serving items that no one else has, or will gladly get you these pieces. The basic big-name brands and patterns are found on almost every island, and now and then you'll find an exclusive in one little shop or even on a cruise ship. For example, I don't know how they do it, but QE2's Spode prices are so low it's laughable. Ships do have good china departments, as do several of the better shopping islands. So if you think the Caribbean is the last place in the world to stock up on your Gianni Versace dinner plates, think again.

Perfume & Cosmetics   It's tricky here. On American brands, savings may only be 10% or 20%. If you're buying a European fragrance, prices may be better in Paris, but if you're not on your way to Paris, prices will be better than at your local department store. The real issue isn't price, but quality and selection. There's more on buying perfume in Chapter 4, "Shopping Strategies."

Liquor   Yes, it really does pay to schlep those heavy bottles around with you. If you're a drinker, stock up now. You'll save 50% on export booze when you buy carefully.

Jewelry & Watches   Beware of the cheaper and all-too-sparkly chains and charms, but many islands do offer excellent prices. To make a purchase like this without sales tax is already saving you money, to say nothing of the 20% to 25% further discount on some high-ticket items. St. Thomas is perhaps the best jewelry island, but many others offer values and discounts. Prices in the Caribbean often can be better than in Hong Kong.

Don't buy:

- Toiletries, sunglasses, or beach items, if you can help it;
- American-manufactured goods, except maybe cosmetics (and be careful on those);
- Ready-to-wear that's not on sale;
- Expensive electronics & cameras (without knowing exactly what you are doing).

CARIBBEAN FAKES

. . . .

If prices are constant, how is it that a friend of yours found a designer handbag on Island A for much less than ever seen on Island B, C, or D? Well, there are several factors, but the most important one is that the handbag is probably a fake.

There are two kinds of fakes going around the Caribbean: bad fakes, which just about anyone

Price Announcement

Now for the Caribbean Basin's big news: Prices are constant. This means prices on perfumes, on crystal, on figurines, on dishes, on cameras, or on any big-ticket item. Prices are "fixed" by distributors and are generally the same on each island throughout the entire region.

Not only does the same bottle of liquor cost the same in every store on one island, chances are excellent that this selfsame bottle of booze costs exactly the same in every store on every island in the Caribbean.

This is *not* true for ready-to-wear or fashion accessories, but it is true for perfume, cosmetics, cameras, china, crystal, and so on.

There's no such thing as Island A having much better prices than Island B, and there is no best place in town to buy a certain item, pricewise. Make your store choice based on selection, service, crowds, or ambience, but not on price, since price doesn't vary.

The one variation on this fixed-price mode is that the Dutch side of St. Maarten prides itself on keeping track of prices in St. Thomas and then lowering prices exactly 10%. However, throughout St. Maarten prices will stay constant.

The only other exception to this is on promotional items. Each store picks different, splashy items with which to attract customers (called loss leaders); they get you in the door and convince you to buy. If an item you want is at a promotional price, you may indeed save a few dollars. I saved $2 on a bottle of Grand Marnier. Keep in mind, though, that for the most part, it doesn't pay to make yourself crazy just to save $2.

Prices may also be less expensive in the mainland United States. You may also get better bargains by mail order and totally forget about shopping in the Caribbean.

can spot; and very sophisticated fakes, sold in reputable-looking stores, with proper-looking tags, boxes, and even felt protective bags. I have seen Gianni Versace, Fendi, and Gucci items that are darn good imitations—and are expensively priced. At the high end, you must be extremely careful because this is where you can get burned the most.

Perhaps my most upsetting story happened in a pierside shop in Martinique (no names, please!) that was on the recommended list provided by the cruise ship and was one of the stores with a so-called guarantee. They had a Gianni Versace evening bag for $468. When I asked about this odd price, the clerk told me it was an uneven number because of the duty-free price. I won't bore you with the details, but here's the bottom line:

- A genuine Gianni Versace bag in a similar style costs $1,500 and a 20% duty-free discount would not have brought the price down to $468;
- The ship's guarantee would not have held in this case because the item is a fraud, which is unfortunately not one of the categories covered in the ship's return policy!

There really are some good buys in the Caribbean. I have seen some sensational savings, and you should indeed be looking forward to shopping on this trip, but please remember this story . . . and don't shop stupid.

A SHORT HISTORY OF SHOPPING IN THE CARIBBEAN

· ·

The Caribbean got its reputation as a shopper's paradise at an early age, starting with the pirates who found their fortunes in the merchant ships traveling from the New World to the Old.

As late as the American Revolutionary War, trading with the Caribbean was still big in what was known as "The Triangle Trade"—Bibles, slaves, and sugar products (molasses and rum) were traded in a triangular route between Africa, the Caribbean, and Boston (via Charleston).

As pirates and slave traders died out, so did a lot of the Caribbean's wealth. Although Puerto Rico developed as a business hub, tourism became the main industry for most other islands.

The Caribbean Basin Recovery Act, passed in the early 1980s, was meant to encourage industry in the islands, but so far has not been very successful. The biggest developments in manufacturing have been in the islands that provide labor to sew already-cut piece goods—thus the Dominican Republic and Jamaica have the most business, at least in the needle trades, while some beading is done in Haiti, and some wet suits are made in Nassau. While there's been talk among garmentos that the Caribbean will replace Hong Kong as the main source for cheap labor, it seems that China is already filling that bill. Then Brazil. But the Caribbean continues to be important to the garment trade.

If you're the factory outlet type, the Caribbean does abound in another type of manufacturing that has nothing to do with clothes but is still related to the history of the islands: There are rum factories galore, and you can visit most of them. This is factory outlet shopping at its finest—most provide free samples to those of drinking age.

Aside from sugar trades and straw markets, whatever shopping exists in the Caribbean (with the exception of diving for sunken treasure) has been artificially transported for the sake of tourists. Cities that host cruise ships have entirely different personalities from those that do not, and a large industry—from selling dolls on docksides to the importing of foreign merchandise—caters to giving the tourists something to buy. It's always easier to sell to a person who is on vacation than to one who is not, so the Caribbean is ready and waiting to take your money.

While some islands have a historical shipping and shopping connection to the countries that colonized them (such as Bermuda with Great Britain), many use their free- or near-free port status to attract goods from all over the world for their visitors.

THE MARKETING OF YOUR MARKETING

· ·

While the Basin is filled with islands, and cruise ships advertise their dedication to finding new ports of call and bringing new experiences to cruising, only a handful of the islands have serious shopping opportunities. Even Cuba, which is currently closed to U.S. citizens and is the dream port of every ship who dares to be the first into town, will offer limited shopping opportunities and few trips to the cigar factory.

People hell-bent on big-time shopping may indeed want to consider some of the 1-week packages that have 3 days in St. Thomas and 4 days on a ship—*Sea Goddess* does one of these and it is fabulous because it also includes St. Barts, a hard-to-get-to but easy-to-shop port of call.

The best shopping is along the route which ships call either Eastern Caribbean or Southern Caribbean; this usually includes Martinique, Barbados, St. Martin / St. Maarten, Antigua, and St. Thomas. These cruises often depart from San Juan, so you get a lot of shopping bang for your buck.

Cruises that stop in Jamaica, the Caymans, and the Western islands do not have the same shopping ops—they're for sportspeople, fishermen, and scuba divers. Cozumel is a shopping delight and Grand Cayman has enough stores to let you stock up on fragrance and wrinkle cream, but frankly, your ship sells everything you need. Mexico has some Mexican flair; otherwise, this is not the big shopping route.

Every now and then, you see an island that looks at marketing statistics, focus groups, and advertising plans and decides to target shoppers. The Bahamas did this in 1992 when they reclassified their duty free; Aruba has just begun to rework its image as the shopping capital of the western and far southern ports. And, of course the U.S. government has gotten into the act, with generous duty-free allowances from the U.S. Virgin Islands, making them always the shopping capital for American citizens.

You don't need a lot of ports, you just need to know what's where and how to tackle it all.

CARIBBEAN BARGAINS

Everything you buy in the Caribbean is not a bargain. Even St. Thomas, which is Deal City, isn't cheap on some items. If you are considering a major purchase—dinner service for 12, for example—do some comparison shopping vis-à-vis Europe and the United States. Since you'll have to ship those 12 place settings, compare shipping and insurance as well. Yes, it's enormous fun to waltz off your ship, glide into a fancy store, and buy something you've dreamed about owning for years. But if you really care about best price, you'll do some homework first.

Gift items and impulse buys are all part of a trip; don't ruin them by pulling out charts and price lists when someone offers to buy you that pretty gold bracelet in the window. (Just say, "Thank you, dear.") Likewise, unless you are doing a big haul on perfumes and cosmetics, it probably doesn't matter if you buy in France or in the Caribbean. But on those once-in-a-lifetime purchases, such as china and crystal, or an important piece of jewelry, know what's happening not only in your hometown at your local retailer, but at big-name American discounters such as **Nat Schwartz.** Call this store at ☎ 800/ 526-1440 and get prices on your patterns, as well as shipping and insurance information. It takes about 3 minutes and will guarantee that you don't get taken in by the islands. For another quote, try **Ross-Simons** at ☎ 800/556-7376.

Oh yes, one more tip: In your research, ask about delivery time. Many of the Caribbean's china dealers do not keep stock! They will order for you at discount prices and come across with a fair shipping and insurance policy, but they will not guarantee delivery . . . which could take 6 to 9 months!

MAIL-ORDER CARIBE
. . . .

If you're not certain about a specific bargain, or you want to save up, or if you simply want to do some armchair Christmas shopping at bargain prices, ask for catalogs and mail-order information from various shops while you're in the islands. These catalogs usually cost a few dollars if you send for them through a magazine ad, but they're free if you collect them in person when you visit the store.

Many of the stores also have toll-free numbers so you can call in your order. Furthermore, you can call in an order and ask for delivery of the packages to separate addresses. If it's a Christmas gift, you may even request Christmas wrap; some stores also have special wedding wrap. It may be difficult for the recipient to return or exchange the gift you've sent from the Caribbean, but if you're sure of your choice (or just don't care), your dollar will go about 25% further.

Among the more famous mail-order and catalog houses is **Little Switzerland,** P.O. Box 930, St. Thomas, U.S.V.I. (☎ 800/524-2010). This is a large, glossy catalog filled with beautiful pictures of name-brand merchandise and fragrance. A separate price sheet keeps you abreast of the latest prices. It should be your bible; order yours before departure.

I also usually keep on hand a catalog from **Domestications** (☎ 800/746-2555) or some other line that sells linens from Asia at great prices, as well as some sort of jewelry catalog or price sheet or ads. For camera prices, I buy one of the photography magazines on the newsstand before I leave—there are a ton of ads in them as well as price lists in the back. I also latch onto the **J&R** catalog from New York City (☎ 800/221-8180), which is great for electronics and cameras. When I'm pricing fragrance by a certain type, I get prices from **Catherine,** my favorite duty free in Paris, by faxing them at ☎ 011/ 33-1-42-61-02-35 (☎ 011/33-1-42-61-02-89).

Remember, not only do you want to compare prices, but you want the bargaining power of being able to say, "Hey, looky here . . ." You want to know what guarantees and customer service are offered to you once you're Stateside, and if these are worth a little extra money compared to service you may (or may not) get from a small island surrounded by blue sea and sharks.

ABOUT ADDRESSES

Very few stores have addresses in the Caribbean. If they do, the address may be Japanese-style—in relation to when the building was built. Thus, number 1 is invariably in the middle of the block somewhere. Since towns are small, everyone knows where these shops are. If you can't find one, ask. We haven't listed building numbers in this book, but don't panic; you won't need them.

SHOPPING HOURS

Hours vary with the culture of the island you are visiting. Contrary to every consumer's basic notion, some islands don't go into overdrive when a ship comes into port—some islands could care less. French islands usually close shop during lunch break (*midi*) and reopen about 2:30pm. American islands and very commercial islands do not close for lunch.

Most stores are open 9am to 7pm, Monday through Saturday. Some will open at 8:30am, especially when a ship is in port. Sunday hours vary.

Sunday Shopping

Most islands have something open on a Sunday, especially if a cruise ship is in port. Note that very often cruises turn around over the weekend, so the Sunday action is in these vital ports and not on other, less trafficked islands.

If you're just visiting one island, on your own, you may find Sunday shopping available in season or not at all, or available but on a diminished scale. Sometimes it is just a straw market or flea market. Sunday in the Caribbean certainly isn't the big day for stores that it can be in the United States.

ISLAND FEVER

You don't cure this one with limes, nor do you need to swig a gallon of grog—but shoppers beware of the dread Island Fever, somewhat related to cabin fever. You get so desperate to buy *something* that you pounce on the nearest store and buy anything at all—including things you'd never buy under normal circumstances.

Cruisers always buy a lot in their first port; but even those shoppers who have spent a few days in their favorite resort on an isolated beach get a little gaga when they get into town. There are some good buys if you shop carefully, but don't buy anything out of boredom or frustration.

SEX AT SEA

I'm sure it's no shock to you that a cruise is considered a romantic getaway by many, and those who aren't in a cabin with double bunk beds and scores of screaming children may actually have something else in mind. Most cruisers have prepared for sexual activity on board, but the cruise line and the stores in port aren't stupid—you may be surprised just how many of them sell massage oil, sexy bathing suits, revealing clothing, and lingerie. People buy, and do, things they might not have dreamed of doing at home. Blame it on La Macarena. You may also want to know that sex toys are less expensive at home than in port.

FOR MORE INFORMATION

There are several organizations and specialty publications that can provide information on the islands, the entire Caribbean Basin, or the cruise lines. Try tourist offices for the islands, and check newsstands for magazines such as *Islands* (which covers islands all over the world, not just in the Caribbean), *Caribbean Travel & Life,* and *Porthole.* Here are a few other sources you might not know about:

- *Affordable Caribbean;* newsletter from the editors of *Caribbean Travel & Life,* P.O. Box 3000, Denville, N.J. 07834.
- Caribbean Vacation Planner; call ☎ 800/365-9999, ext. 209 for information from the Caribbean Coalition for Tourism.

Electronically Yours: Relevant Web Sites

Antigua & Barbuda:
www.interknowledge.com/Antigua-barbuda

Bahamas: **www.interknowledge.com**

Bermuda: **www.ibl.bm.**

Caribbean Information Office:
www.caribbeans.com

Caribbean Tourism Office:
www.travelfile.com/get?cto

French West Indies:
www.crl.com/~philip/fwi.html

U.S. Virgin Islands: **www.usvi.net/**

CELEBRATE AT SEA

. . . .

If you are celebrating a special event at sea, tell your travel agent, who can arrange for a cake to be brought to the table and may even get you invited to the captain's table. Also, each cruise line has a shopping service whereby you can order gifts, wine or champagne, or treats sent to the cabin either for yourself or for friends and family traveling on their own cruises. Prices are usually in the $25 to $35 range; if a brochure detailing these services is not in the package with your cruise documents, call your cruise line's customer service number and ask about on-board gifts and goodies.

You may also rent a tuxedo at sea; call ☎ 800/ 551-5091. Prices are about $75 for a 1-week rental that includes coat, pants, two shirts, cummerbund, bow tie, studs, and cufflinks. Black formal shoes cost an additional $10 per week; $5 buys you a pair of black formal socks that you get to keep!

Charge It!

And while we're talking about on-board services, this is the best time to warn you about how easy it is to spend money on board a ship. Of course, you're going to go to the duty free and the perfume shop as soon as they open, of course you need some logo merchandise—for yourself and for gifts—these are givens. Done. Charge it. But what you might not realize is that the ship charges for just about everything else, and that bar and service tips are automatically included on bills. I can't tell you how many cruises I've been on where I added another 10% to 15% to the bar bill or the manicurist chit!

Also note that almost every ship features a "drink of the day," which is a lot less expensive than the usual on-board cocktails. If you're flexible in your drinking habits, check the ship's program or ask your cocktail waiter what the drink of the day is. On Caribbean cruises, these are almost always variations of rum drinks so you won't really have to break stride if you can handle a slightly different one each day.

Serious drinkers, of course, know to bring their own bottle with them and to drink in their cabins. Also bring mixers, soft drinks, and even bottles of water, since ships charge $2.50 for each little plastic bottle of water and $1.50 for each canned soft drink.

I can remember desperately trying to get off the ship in one port to be quite annoyed that the gangway was clogged with an incredible mob scene. What was going on? The ship had a cart *selling* bottled water right at the door!

I've been on plenty of ships where they give away the bottled water, they give you towelettes and a spritzer and every ammenity known to man, but most of the mass market ships charge for everything! In some cases you may be charged automatically, or unexpectedly asked to produce your cruise card (your on-board credit card) to pay for a drink you have already swallowed that you thought was free!

Wine is rarely included with your meal; many ships have a week-long package that allows you to save money by buying what's named a "Wine & Dine" deal. Ask about it. If you bring your own wine on board, or buy it in a port—which is especially fun in a French port—expect to be charged a corkage fee (usually $10 per bottle) for having that wine served at dinner.

Wine Etiquette & Payments

I can't tell you how many people ask me about this. As noted, wine is not usually included with the meal. Here's how it goes: You're probably at a table with several other people, who may well be strangers if you are not with a prebooked group or an entire table of family members. Quite probably, you will get a free bottle of wine sent to you by your travel agent.

Whether it's the free bottle or one you've ordered for yourselves, are you supposed to share with the other people at the table, and to what extent?

So, most tables break down very quickly—even on the first night—into two types: the couple who will host the wine for the entire table for a night, and the couple who makes it quite clear that they don't share, in order to eliminate any financial risks.

The basic rule of thumb is that if you accept more than one glass of wine, you should "pay back" at some point. If you are worried about being obligated, simply don't accept hospitality from another passenger.

But wait: Single women may expect gentlemen to pick up the tab, though this is trickier in modern times than it used to be—if you're panicked, ask.

PHONING HOME

. . . .

Like every place else in the world, the Caribbean has changed many of its area codes. Old guidebooks may not have up-to-date phone numbers; ask your ship's concierge or information desk if you're making a local phone call.

Some of the newer codes: Antigua (and Barbuda), 268; Bahamas, 242; Barbados, 246; Cayman Islands, 345; Puerto Rico, 787. If all the numbers you have listed are 809 area codes, be suspicious. Some are still 809, but many have changed.

While you can certainly call any place in the world from the telephone in your cabin, you may not want to when you see the prices—which usually run $15 a minute.

Instead, buy a phone card from your cruise ship (Princess sells these), use U.S. direct phones located in pier terminals, or use the access code of your favorite long-distance carrier. My best trick is to use my **France Telecom** phone card on French islands. Of course, you need to buy a France Telecom card in a store or newsagent or have one left over from a trip to France.

If you need to send a fax, it will also cost about $15 per minute from the ship. Instead, check out fax services in pier terminals, or walk into any hotel in town and ask them to send the fax for you. While there is a charge for this, it's not anywhere near $15 a minute!

PRECRUISE BOOKINGS

If you plan on renting a car on any (or all) of the islands or spending a half day at a hotel property on any specific island (yes, you can indeed do this!), try to book ahead and have paperwork with you so that you can confirm that your plans have been made and prices established. Sometimes a few details slip through the cracks between Miami and the Caribbean Basin. Prices for these things are often less expensive when done ahead of time from the U.S., so go for it and enhance that trip of yours. Then sit back, shop a little, and enjoy yourself. Remember, we're gonna limbo tonight.

Chapter Three

· · · · · · · · ·

PORTS AT A GLANCE

In this chapter, I've compiled essential information for eight of the Caribbean's most popular port cities—all in an easy-to-read, at-a-glance format. I'll map out the main shopping drags, tell you how much time to spend in each port, and recommend lunch spots as well as other don't-miss daytime diversions. Note that the store hours I list are generally valid Monday through Friday. Weekend store hours fluctuate with the season and often depend on whether or not a ship is in port.

St. John's, Antigua

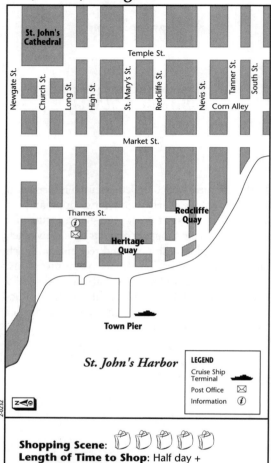

St. John's Cathedral

Temple St.

Newgate St.
Church St.
Long St.
High St.
St. Mary's St.
Redcliffe St.
Nevis St.
Tanner St.
South St.

Corn Alley

Market St.

Thames St.

ⓘ
✉

Redcliffe Quay

Heritage Quay

Town Pier

St. John's Harbor

LEGEND

Cruise Ship Terminal 🚢
Post Office ✉
Information ⓘ

2-0232

Shopping Scene: 🛍️🛍️🛍️🛍️🛍️
Length of Time to Shop: Half day +
Docking to Shopping Ratio: Walking distance
Shopping Hours: 9am–6pm; some stores
  open at 8:30am when ships are in port
Lunch: Return to the ship for the free lunch;
  it's too convenient not to take advantage
  of your ship facilities
Best Stores: Body Shop, Jacaranda, Casa del
  Habano, Base, Caribelle Batik, Thousand Flowers,
  Decibels, Gold Smitty
Amusing: Street vendors that line Market
  Street selling crafts and art from boxes
Don't Miss: Inner courtyard of Nelson's Dock

Nassau, Bahamas

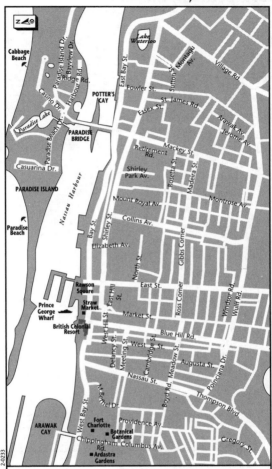

Shopping Scene: 🛍🛍

Length of Time to Shop: Half Day +

Docking to Shopping Ratio: Walking distance

Shopping Hours: 9am–5pm; early close on Thursdays (noon)

Lunch: Eat the free lunch on the ship or head out to one of the hotels such as Chris Blackwell's Compass Point, at Love Beach

Best Stores: Balmain Antiques; Amos Ferguson Studio

Amusing: Straw Market

Don't Miss: Fruit and fish market under the bridge

Bridgetown, Barbados

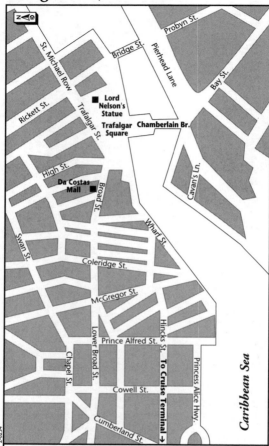

Shopping Scene:

Length of Time to Shop: One hour to half day

Docking to Shopping Ratio: Excellent mall at cruise terminal; distance to downtown walkable but not in heat, so taxi there

Shopping Hours: 9am–5pm weekdays; 8am–1pm Saturdays

Lunch: Splurge on lunch at one of the luxury hotels on the Glitter Coast; Sandy Lane is my choice—or eat at Mount Gay Rum Factory

Best Stores: Gatsby's, Mount Gay Factory Store

Amusing: Chattel-house style mini-malls such as one located at rear of cruise pier

Don't Miss: Mount Gay

Fort-de-France, Martinique

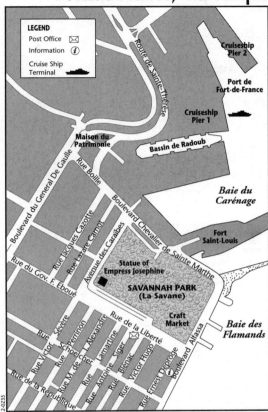

Shopping Scene: 🛍️🛍️🛍️
Length of Time to Shop: Half day
Docking to Shopping Ratio: Small strip of
  stores at pier; taxi to downtown shopping
  in Fort-de-France
Shopping Hours: 9am–12:30pm and 2:30–7pm
  (only a few stores stay open during lunch)
Lunch: Late lunch on board if you're finished
  shopping, or at Lina's Café for a quick bite
Best Stores: Roger Albert; Ginger;
  Pharmacie Sainte Rose
Amusing: Coco Cadeaux, funky little TT (tourist
  trap) for crafts and local art; Market stalls and TTs
  in La Savane, the park
Don't Miss: Backstreets of downtown and real
  people shopping with a Caribbean French twist

San Miguel de Cozumel, Mexico

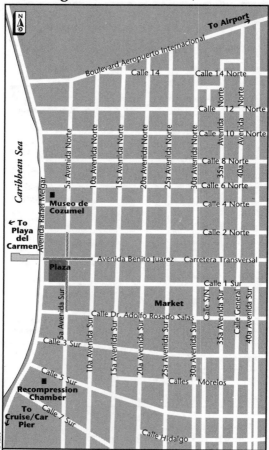

Shopping Scene:
Length of Time to Shop: All day
(beware of siesta)
Docking to Shopping Ratio: Take taxi from
international pier
Shopping Hours: 9am–1pm and 3pm–7pm;
some TTs open nonstop
Lunch: Carlos & Charlie's on the *malecón*
Best Stores: Los Cinco Soles, Polo/
Ralph Lauren, Explora
Amusing: Frog kitsch sold in TTs on *malecón*
Don't Miss: Ave. 5 Norte for craft shops

Old San Juan, Puerto Rico

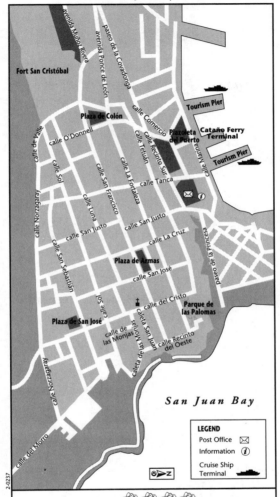

Shopping Scene: 🛍️🛍️🛍️🛍️
Length of Time to Shop: Full day
Docking to Shopping Ratio: Walking distance
Shopping Hours: 9am–6pm
Lunch: El Convento Hotel (on the patio)
Best Stores: Polo/Ralph Lauren Factory Store,
   Sunny Caribbee, Pusser's
Amusing: Street vendors at plaza near
   tourist office and pier
Don't Miss: Factory outlet stores on Calle del Cristo

Philipsburg, St. Maarten

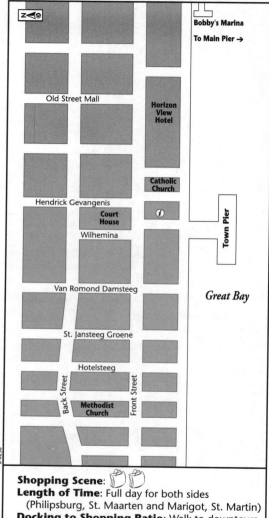

Old Street Mall

Horizon View Hotel

Bobby's Marina

To Main Pier →

Catholic Church

Hendrick Gevangenis

Court House

i

Wilhemina

Town Pier

Van Romond Damsteeg

Great Bay

St. Jansteeg Groene

Hotelsteeg

Back Street

Front Street

Methodist Church

2-0238

Shopping Scene:

Length of Time: Full day for both sides
  (Philipsburg, St. Maarten and Marigot, St. Martin)

Docking to Shopping Ratio: Walk to downtown
  Philipsburg; taxi to Marigot

Shopping Hours: Dutch (St. Maarten) side:
  8:30am–5pm; French (St. Martin) side:
  9am–12:30pm and 2:30pm–7pm

Lunch: Marigot

Best Stores: Little Switzerland (both sides)

Amusing: Guavaberry Liqueur Shop, Philipsburg

Don't Miss: Old Street, Philipsburg

Charlotte Amalie, St. Thomas

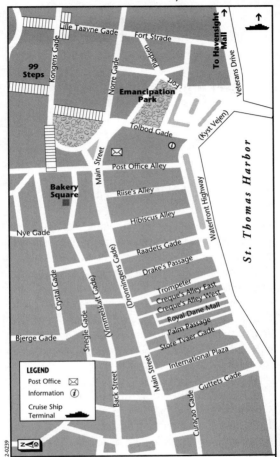

Shopping Scene:

Length of Time to Shop: Full day

Docking to Shopping Ratio: Havensight Mall at cruise piers; taxi to downtown Charlotte Amalie

Shopping Hours: 9am–5pm

Lunch: Consider returning to ship to unload if burdened by packages and enjoy quick, free lunch or try La Scala, in town

Best Stores: A.H. Riise, Pampered Pirate, H. Stern

Amusing: Flea Market at Emancipation Square selling designer fakes

Don't Miss: Side alleys such as Hibiscus Alley

Chapter Four

. . . .

SHOPPING STRATEGIES

SAVINGS AT SEA

. . . .

Of course you expect to find some savings when you shop on the islands, but smart shoppers will begin to save before they even book their cruises. With more and more berths appearing on ships, with bigger and bigger ships being built, there's tremendous competition out there and a good bit of space that you can maybe have, for a song. Prices are actually falling, so drop anchor in some of these savings and have more to spend when you get to port!

STRATEGIES BEFORE YOU BOOK

. . . .

The cruise lines offer myriad discounts, including special rates for: people who have been on the line before (offers come to you, unsolicited, through the mail); those who bring along children with two fully paid tickets; those who book 6, 9, or 12 months in advance; and those who are willing to try a new ship—especially on its maiden voyage.

There are other discounts or incentives if you book another cruise on the same line while you're on board your current cruise, more deals if it's a special occasion—you name it, and there's a discount! It may be only 5%, but often you can combine several discounts to get some real relief. Yep, two-for-one deals and other breaks actually can bring the price down by half.

Before you get all carried away with a cruise discounter, know what the commonly offered cruise line discounts are so you can decide if you're really getting a bargain or not. Discounters sometimes offer the same old discount anyone can get . . . or even less of a deal. The real savings go to those who can run the numbers from several different sources and compare not only price but the thrown-in extras.

Read on for assorted strategies and savings.

STRATEGIES TOWARD SAVINGS

. . . .

There are two types of discounters in the business: travel clubs, of which you must be a member; and wholesalers, who usually just deal with cruise business and do an enormous volume of business with a number of lines. If you know you want to go on a cruise, but you don't know which line or which ports, you'll do best to investigate wholesalers. If you don't care where you go, a club will probably offer the best buys.

If you have a favorite cruise line, compare its discount offerings to those in a discount packager's catalog (chances are, they'll match).

With the firms whose main business is cruises, you'll find a well-organized, although slightly aggressive, pattern of service. You'll be able to call these brokers toll free and ask them questions; they'll track down information for you and call you back.

A few firms will not do business with you until they have sent you a catalog, but that's okay—you want as many catalogs as possible so you can compare prices.

Cruise Market Place Discounts on all cruise lines, with routes all over the world; call for a list of their discounts, which are as much as 50% off list price; ☎ 800/826-4333.

CUC International Travel   This is a club that sells last-minute packages (4 weeks, or less, before the ship departs). They have package trips everywhere, cruise and noncruise, but you must join up. Write to: Stand-Buys Ltd., P.O. Box 1015, Trumbull, CT 06611 (☎ 800/255-0200), for a free fact kit. Cruise bargains can be 50%. Every now and then we call their hotline number to find out what's available and discover cruises at more or less regularly discounted prices, with or without airfare. Cruises that were $1,000 won't be slashed as low as $299, but may be $499. A hotline number is provided to members only, but once you have the hotline you call for a taped recording of the latest deals.

Spur-of-the-Moment Cruises   Call for reservations (☎ 800/343-1991), or try the hotline telling you just what the bargains are! Again, bargains are the standard discount. The hotline number is ☎ 310/521-1060; there's no membership fee. Also, "spur of the moment" may be a misnomer—in January, they were offering May dates and even some October dates.

Golden Age Travelers   You must be 50 or over to join this club, but there are good senior citizen's deals on cruises; call ☎ 800/258-8880.

Don Ton Travel   This is a cruise broker specializing in luxury cruises, which can be bought right up until the date of departure—some stop selling 30 days before the sailing date, but not Don Ton. They have deals to the Caribbean as well as Europe and around the world; they're quite impressive. Call ☎ 800/318-1818.

CONSORTIUMS R US

I am personally associated with a consortium, so I have learned a little about this, and I find it pretty amazing. Let's go to the head of the class because you may have never known about a consortium or the kinds of deals that await.

Okay, all those travel agents are out there, some big, some small. When they band together and form a consortium, they get better deals because of the strength in numbers. Of the five or seven really big consortiums, I work with **Giants** (☎ 800/442-6871), which is made up of 1,900 individual agencies.

Consortiums pressure the cruise lines to grant them concessions in price and perks for travel during the trip in order to bring better deals to their clients.

When you buy a cruise from a Giants agency— or any other consortium for that matter—you pay a flat price for many "inclusives," so you're getting a discount on the fare and then some extras, such as prepaid gratuities and possibly a shore excursion or an exclusive event or whatever it is that the consortium specializes in. **API Travel Consultants** (☎ 212/759-8940), which is the single fanciest group at the highest end, usually offers their cruise passengers an exclusive shore excursion; that has been their niche, or extra service, for years.

Now, Giants also offers shore tours or exclusive events on some of their cruise ships. (Book one that I'm on, and you'll get me thrown in for free!) Ask each agency you call for exact details on the extras and perks, and then figure out the value they offer. If tips, port charges, etc. are not included in the deal you're considering, do your paperwork and make sure you're figuring all expenses and all possible savings before you rule out the benefits of a consortium.

Once I was involved in a conversation with several passengers on board Crystal's *Symphony,* and each person told me a different price and a different package for his add-on hotel, ship-to-airport or hotel transfers, excursions, souvenirs, and on-board gifts (such as wine, champagne, and cash to spend on board—yes, cash!). You'd be shocked at what's negotiable out there, especially at the high end of the scale.

CRUISE SPECIALTY AGENCY STRATEGIES

Some agencies just sell cruises, claiming that by specializing they really know the ships, the ports, and what's right for their clients on an individual basis. A few you might want to call when you are comparison shopping:

Cruise Vacations, ☎ 800/631-3636

Cruises International, ☎ 800/255-7447

The Cruise Line Inc., ☎ 800/777-0707

Cruise Value Center, ☎ 800/231-7447

THE MOSCOW RULE OF SHOPPING

If you are new to Born to Shop, then you should know one of my most basic strategies—The Moscow Rule of Shopping. This is for travelers anywhere, even to Miami and the Caribbean. You simply pretend that you're shopping in Moscow, where you know that if you don't buy something immediately, it won't be there when you come back.

While a few things keep popping up in the islands (if I see one more Sunglass Hut I may scream), for the most part, if you love it, buy it and don't look back. Prices are fixed just about everywhere, so it's really a question of selection. Buy it or forget it.

THE LENINGRAD RULE OF CRUISING

If you're going on a cruise to many different islands and you want bargains, but you're confused as to what to buy in which port or when to pounce and when to go soft, step this way. The Leningrad Rule of Cruising is very simple: Aruba, St. Martin/St. Maarten, and St. Thomas.

If you aren't going to Aruba or to St. Martin/St. Maarten, it usually comes down to St. Thomas.

St. Martin/St. Maarten has two (Marigot and Philipsburg) very shopable cities and the best selection of European merchandise in the Caribbean. St. Thomas gives you an additional $600 duty-free allowance for buying there and then a 5% discount on the next $1,000 worth of goods.

St. Thomas has the retailer's mentality. Many islands don't understand what the sophisticated shopper wants or needs; many vendors on the islands think it's their right to cheat you, or that you buy from them and make them rich—this manifests itself in a bad attitude. St. Thomas is ready and waiting for you. St. Maarten is usually cheaper on ready-to-wear, cameras, and electronics, but does not have the same serve-you-with-style attitude.

Final corollary to the Leningrad Rule of Cruising: If you are buying primitive Haitian art, consider buying it at Labadee (an exclusive Royal Caribbean Cruise Line port). Very few other ports sell it, and the prices in the market in Labadee are controlled, so you don't get ripped off.

According to the Leningrad Rule of Cruising, don't follow the traditional cruisers' blow-it-all-in-the-first-port pattern. Most people on a cruise spend the most money in the first port the ship stops in. They can't help it; after being at sea for 24 hours, they run onto shore and buy anything that moves, or gathers dust. But look at this coldly—why do most cruise companies route the trip so you stop at Charlotte Amalie on the last stop? They save the best for last, of course.

THE *WHEEL OF FORTUNE* RULE OF SHOPPING
. . . .

Perhaps you haven't seen as many TV game shows as I have, but if you've paid attention to them at all, you've noticed that the winners on *Wheel of Fortune* (and other shows, too) have to spend their earnings on a galaxy of prizes with prices attached to them. God knows where they find these prices, but they seem outrageously expensive!

Okay, here's the catch: the suggested manu-
facturer's retail price for game-show prizes is *not*
for real. Remember this when you shop in the
Caribbean.

While advertisements, shopping guides (especially
the kind that are fancy forms of advertising), and
even cruise directors may tell you that prices are
50% less than in the United States, we beg you to
use your head. Unless you fall into a lucky sale,
which thousands of people will do during the course
of the year, you will not find 50% (or more) savings
on anything except liquor.

The average savings in the Caribbean is 20% to
25%. End of story. Tack on sales tax to inflate the
savings, but don't beat it to death.

Beware of anyone who promises you more than
a 50% savings on nonsale merchandise of anything
except liquor and, maybe, linens from China.

THE RULE OF THE DOLLAR

. . . .

When calculating prices (and savings) on European
imports, the savings for Americans are directly related to the strength, or weakness, of the U.S. dollar. When the dollar is strong, you'll find excellent
bargains on European imports when they're bought
in their home countries or in many of the Caribbean free or near-free ports. When the dollar is weak,
savings shrivel up.

STRATEGIES FOR DUTY-FREE
& TAX-FREE SHOPPING

. . . .

The notion of duty-free shopping in the Caribbean
is the area's major "gotcha." Very few of the islands
are actually free ports—and that includes the city of
Freeport! It's just that the words "free port" and
"duty free" are so romantic, they seem to sell so

much merchandise, they make such music in our ears . . . we just can't resist them. In the old days, before there were discounters on every highway and factory outlet malls near every byway, people counted on saving money through duty-free sources. Kids, that was years ago.

Nowadays, duty free is an enormous business—and a very profitable one at that. I love duty free and I feel very much a part of its success, but I don't promise you that duty free is the bargain haven that you anticipate.

Before I give you the lowdown, please remember one thing: Revlon.

At my local drugstore, a bottle of Revlon nail polish costs about $3. This is not a discounted price and is basically the going price anywhere in the U.S. At duty-free stores in the Caribbean, the same Revlon nail polish sells for about $4!

If it's sold at a duty free, why isn't it cheaper?

Well, some islands (or countries) charge absolutely no duty whatsoever on imports or exports. These islands are known as free ports. The best-known free port of the Caribbean is St. Martin/ St. Maarten—both sides are true free ports. Many islands (or countries) charge no duty on some items. Most frequently the items they do not charge duty on are the ones they plan to sell to tourists; so their laws are built accordingly, allowing for luxury items such as perfumes or china and crystal to enter (and leave) without duty. Every now and then, an island even changes laws in order to increase tourism, just as the Bahamas did in 1992 when they did away with 11 categories of goods that were previously taxed.

In a few islands, the island itself is not duty free but there are zones where goods are technically held in bond and do not enter the country. These goods are sold outside the country, from airports or ports so taxes are never added on. Such zones exist at La Zona Franca in Santo Domingo, Dominican Republic; Pointe Seraphine, on the island of St. Lucia; and at Porlamar, which is part of Margarita Island off the coast of Venezuela.

Stricter in-bond shopping policies are offered in Bermuda, Jamaica, Trinidad, and Tobago where the goods are held with specialty dealers or warehouses and sent directly to your plane or ship so that they cannot enter the real people part of the destination.

THE SALES TAX TRICK

Now then, when a Caribbean store tells you to expect savings of up to 30% over Stateside prices, what they often mean is that retail price is 20% less than in the United States, and you pay no sales tax.

There are many ways (legal ways) to avoid paying sales tax in the U.S., so sniff out this kind of information carefully. On the other hand, if you are buying a lipstick or some small item that offers you a marginal savings from the U.S. price, the lack of sales tax becomes an added benefit that could very well double your savings.

No one is going to phone out of state for a lipstick in the U.S., so the 10% savings over retail added to your sales tax, if you live in New York State, gives you a total savings of 18$\frac{1}{4}$%. New York has the highest sales tax, but you get the idea.

When a Caribbean retailer judges a saving, he is also figuring from top-of-the-line retail prices, and he is boasting the largest possible margin of savings.

VALUE-ADDED TAX (VAT)

No Caribbean island except Martinique has value-added taxes, so you need not apply for a VAT refund, or *détaxe,* as you would when leaving a European country. Since Martinique does have TVA (which is the French abbreviation for VAT), please see page 174 for what to do there.

U.S. TAX STRATEGIES

· ·

You may purchase in the islands on a duty-free, tax-free basis, but when you return to the United States, you are required to pay duty on your purchases if you exceed your duty-free allowance.

However, many Caribbean islands have either GSP (Generalized System of Preferences) or CBI (Caribbean Basin Initiative) status, so that goods made on the island—no matter how expensive—can be imported to the U.S. totally without duty.

To qualify under the GSP, 35% or more of the item must be made on that island. So you will not pay duty on arts and handicrafts, no matter how expensive they are; local toilet waters or perfumes are duty free; and so on.

Also note, per below, that the customs and duties are more liberal on a visit to the Caribbean than to other parts of the world, and the U.S. does offer a very special shoppers delight for those who are considering spending some big bucks in the U.S. Virgin Islands.

U.S. CUSTOMS AND DUTIES

· ·

Because the United States gives a special shopper's break to those people who visit the U.S. Virgin Islands, the laws on customs and duties can be confusing—especially to a person who has been to several ports. Also note that NAFTA is killing the Caribbean Basin trade-wise, and President Clinton is trying to pass new laws to make more goods from the Caribbean duty free to the U.S. so Caribbean businesses don't go broke.

As we go to press, these are the rules of the game. An American citizen usually qualifies to bring $400 worth of goods into the U.S. on a duty-free basis if he or she has been out of the country more than 48 hours and has not taken advantage of this offer within the previous 30 days. *However,* a visitor to the Caribbean may bring in $600 worth of goods. Ta da!

If you visit the U.S. Virgin Islands, you're allowed an additional $600 duty-free allowance. This means you can enter the U.S. with $600 worth of goods from the other islands and $600 from the Virgin Islands, for a total of $1,200. Elsewhere in the world, when you go over the $400 allowance, you pay a flat 10% duty on the next $1,000 worth of goods, or $100. Thereafter you are charged at regular rates per item. However, for travel to the U.S. Virgin Islands, you are charged a flat 5% on the next $1,000—that's just $50!

There are special duties on liquor brought out of the U.S. Virgin Islands: You may bring in five bottles of liquor duty free, or six bottles duty free provided one of them is produced in the Virgin Islands. If the booze is bought elsewhere (say, Martinique, because you wanted a premium French label), then you are allowed the same old regular allowance, which is just one bottle!

You may also send yourself, duty free, one package a day worth $50 from the islands, or one package a day worth $100 from the U.S. Virgin Islands. Since the post office is located right in downtown Charlotte Amalie, consider mailing smaller items directly home. Or ask the store to ship for you; they will even stagger the days on which packages are sent out.

MONEY STRATEGIES

Many of the Caribbean Islands trade in the U.S. dollar, and some of the Caribbean Islands (Puerto Rico, U.S. Virgin Islands) are actually part of the United States and use U.S. currency. Other islands will insist you change your money.

If you can avoid changing money, do so. That's why God invented credit cards.

Many islands have their own currency, but because they do such a big business with tourists, will take U.S. dollars. If you insist that you have no other money, you can usually pay in dollars. Your change, however, will be in local currency.

Prices on goods are often marked in several prices, all shown with a $ sign—this will leave you totally confused. Ask the store which currency the prices are marked in, or which of the color-coded numbers is the U.S. dollar price. (Very often prices will be written in blue, black, and red ink—in local dollars, U.S. dollars, and perhaps francs or marks or florins or guilders.) When you pay for an item, especially if the purchase is by credit card, verify what currency you are being charged in.

I admit to being so paranoid that I write initials, such as "U.S." on the charge slip.

If you feel that you must change money, change small amounts of money, and try not to get stuck with leftover money. Or convert into currencies that you know you can use again, such as French francs.

Ask if there is a commission for changing money. I was once charged $10 commission in the Santo Domingo airport for changing a $100 American Express traveler's check. See if I go back there again soon!

Usually cruise ships have a "bureau de change" for changing money.

Do financial conversions between currencies when you have a choice of paying either one. Since I always keep a stock of French francs, I'm prepared for French ports or don't mind exchanging money and being stuck with leftover bills or change. There are few other currencies that I can say that about, especially in the Caribbean. I certainly don't hang on to pesos!

On some islands, they like to predetermine the price of the dollar, so if you want them to take U.S. dollars you must abide by their artificial exchange rate. *C'est la vie.*

If you're connecting home through Miami, note that whatever leftover currency you have after your trip can be converted back to U.S. dollars in the Miami airport at one of several different change booths. They do charge a commission for this, but I'd rather have $6 American than $10 Dominican currency. Miami banks are more familiar with the numerous Caribbean and South American currencies than other banks; those in the airport are there to provide this service and are far easier to deal with than your hometown bank.

If you are going on a cruise, it's very likely that you can make do without changing any currency at all. At first that might sound silly, but think it through:

- Tours are paid for on board, in dollars;
- Even if you aren't going on a tour, shopping districts are often within walking distance, eliminating the need for taxi fares or bus tokens;
- Ships often run free shuttle service into town, so you have no transportation costs when it's too far to walk;
- Most stores take credit cards;
- Many vendors will accept U.S. dollars.

STRATEGIES FOR THE SHOPPING PARENT

Can a shopping parent go on a cruise—or hole up in a resort—with child (or children) in tow and still be able to get in some decent shopping time? Don't snicker; I thought it was a very important question.

If you aren't on a cruise, a good choice for you is **Club Med** (☎ 800/CLUB-MED in the U.S.). Some Club Meds have children's camps, so you can park the kids for the day and escape for an island shopping spree. If you want to do this, plan ahead and make sure you choose an island with the combination of camp and decent shopping. "All our clubs have shopping nearby," says my friend Edwina at Club Med, "otherwise people would kill us."

Family-oriented cruise ships also specialize in child care, not only on board while you're at sea, but for some days in port. Some kids' programs actually take the tots on a shore excursion, for free! Even if you have to pay for it, if they have the kids in hand, and you're free to shop for half a day or so, don't knock it.

During high season, many hotels specialize in kiddie programs, so you can add on to your cruise, stay a few days at a resort, and then get in some shopping on your own. At San Juan's Caribe Hilton there's a *free* day-camp program the Hilton provides for kids 4 to 13—I'm talking supervised beach time, arts and crafts, field trips, and sporting events as well as a free T-shirt. Camp is offered during the summer and holiday seasons from 9:30am until 4pm.

STRATEGIES WHEN ONE SHOPS, THE OTHER DOESN'T

· ·

If you're sick and tired of those trips where you shop and your husband paces back and forth in front of the store, making you a nervous wreck and totally ruining your good time, we have a few suggestions for you: Book a cruise, with the understanding that your man will return to the ship when he gets bored, leaving you free to browse. There isn't enough to do in any port that you can't finish your shopping in a matter of hours.

Book a cruise that's tied in with a sporting event, or that offers a golf or tennis package. Most cruise lines will book tennis courts or greens time for you, but you must request these bookings when you book your passage (or, at least, from the tour desk before you arrive in port). There are theme cruises, many of which are tied to sports, that will more than keep the menfolk happy while the women sneak off to shop. **Norwegian Cruise Lines** does several cruises with famous football and/or baseball players on board; **Royal Caribbean** is associated with the Professional Golf Association (PGA).

Book a day-trip for yourself to an island where the shopping is better or different from where you are. Sometimes it's fun just to go off on your own for a 1-day adventure, even if you don't buy that much or save anything.

Go to a Club Med that is on an island with good shopping and some sort of transportation that will get you to that shopping (see Strategies for the Shopping Parent, page 56).

If you must taxi some distance to and from town, organize a group of other shoppers so you can split the fare.

Choose hotels or resorts with shuttle services to shopping areas, like those in Bermuda. If you stay at the Southampton Princess you can take a free ferry into town for a day's shopping. The nonshopper of the family might not want to stay at the Hamilton Princess, which is in the heart of the shopping district, but you won't suffer from this decision and will pay no extra for transportation to the stores. Most big-time resorts provide guests with free van service into town, returning late in the afternoon. Sam Lord's in Barbados and the Princess in Curaçao do this; L'Habitation in St. Martin offers van service to Marigot, but just during high season. If you think you'll go nuts without easy access to a town and its stores, ask about shuttle services and their cost before you book a resort.

ON-SHIP STRATEGY

All cruise ships have stores on board. The average ship used to have four shops, which sold everything from toiletries to the kind of cruisewear you'd need if you forgot anything. You'd also find a liquor shop and a gift shop that sells watches, cameras, jewelry, perfume, and some cosmetics.

The new breed of cruise ships, however, have created virtual on-board malls. The *QE2* may have lost Harrods, but just about everything else is now available on board, including very upscale shops selling more than the junk you might be expecting.

There's always what the ship calls a "logo shop," which sells all sorts of merchandise bearing the ship's name—pens, place mats, T-shirts, etc. More often than not there's a branch of H. Stern, the most famous jeweler in the Caribbean, who actually got his start on cruise ships. There's an all-purpose store, often run by one of the merchant princes of the duty-free world, and then some individual spaces are leased to big names such as Bally, Spode, and more.

To understand the reasoning behind a ship's stores, you must understand how a cruise ship works. Basically, with the cost of overhead, advertising, and pretty brochures, cruise companies break even on the expenses of the ship and the take from tickets. They make their real money on the drinks. They also make very serious money from gambling concessions, from which they get a percentage of the take.

After that, the ship will offer services to encourage you to not only enjoy yourself, but spend your leisure dollars. The ship wants you to shop and to "spa yourself" right on board.

Meanwhile, they have a problem: Law demands on-board concessions close down when the ship is in territorial waters, so when you come into port, ship stores will be closed. With limited hours available for shopping, how can a ship shop make money?

Simple: by offering great prices.

Don't be surprised if prices for the same items in the island stores are cheaper *on board your ship*. Also expect your ship to agree to match the prices that you find on shore, or they'll refund your purchase.

Now a cruise ship might not have the same selection as an island, but it does have the same brands and the same kinds of merchandise. If you're buying basics, or if you're the type who wants to shop quickly and be done with it, the smartest thing to do is to shop the ship and write down prices.

Take your price list with you into port. Compare prices, then buy the item at the ship shop (if it wins the bidding war) on the way home when the shop will be open the final day at sea.

Generally speaking, if the ship has a duty free that sells booze (not all of them do!), liquor will be less expensive than the regular listed price on an island, but more expensive than the in-bond price. If you are buying one bottle, a savings of $2 might be meaningless.

As for perfume and cosmetics, the prices should be exactly the same on the ship as in any duty free. In fact, the company that runs the duty free for the ship may also run the duty free at the airport. The biggest problem with perfume in the Caribbean, and I have written more extensively later in this chapter about fragrance, is actually selection, not price. Because of the limited amount of shelf space on the ship and possibly the limited number of connections the ship has through its duty-free distributor, only certain brands will be carried. When you ask for one they don't have, they'll try to convince you to buy something they do have.

Ships also all have photo shops on board; usually you can buy film, batteries, one-use cameras, and also buy your on-board photographs. Often these photos are made into gimmick items, such as keychains or coffee mugs, T-shirts, or the like. Film is expensive on ships and in port, but it's usually more fairly priced on board. That's not saying much, but if you are between the devil and the deep blue sea, and you have to pick one, just sign for it; it won't be so painful. Naturally, it's better to stock up before you leave home.

LUCKY CABIN STRATEGY

Many of the stores in any given port will add to the fun of being in port by the posting of a lucky cabin number. If you have the key to the cabin so designated, you get a gift. It might be a $10 T-shirt or a $100 vase. Usually the numbers are in the back of a store so you have to walk through the whole store to get to it. You must declare the gift with your U.S. Customs allowance.

BACK-TO-BACK HOPPING & SHOPPING

. . . .

In the 1950s, island-hopping was considered very chic—you get on an airplane and jump from city to city. It may be fun, but it's difficult for the serious shopper to load up and keep getting on and off planes. A cruise is the easiest (and possibly least expensive) way to see and do it all.

If you want to take in as many ports and experience as many shopping opportunities as possible, consider booking two 1-week cruises back-to-back. (If you book them on the same cruise line, expect special rates and solid discounts.) When investigating this, just make sure you're going in and out of the same port city!

One other tip: By using San Juan as your point of embarkation, you are already in the Caribbean and can get to other islands and stores all the quicker. If the cruise fare doesn't include airfare, don't be frightened away—it's often no more expensive to fly to San Juan than to Miami.

CONSUMING STRATEGIES

. . . .

Before coming to port, every ship offers a free spiel by the cruise director or by a new breed of consultant, the port lecturer. The cruise director is employed by the ship, whereas the port lecturer is employed by a firm with ties to shipping firms and to individual retailers. Their job, no matter which one does it, is to tell you what to expect in port and to give you a rundown of the shopping opportunities. Many of them do this speech as a "show and tell" presentation with either real merchandise or with slides.

You'll probably find these lectures informative and may even plan your time on board to make sure you don't miss them.

Cruise directors may give rather pat little speeches, peppered with clichés and jokes they know will work. They are still good for basic information about the island. If you cannot attend the speech in person, it's always broadcast on the ship's radio or TV channel, so you can listen to it in your cabin.

Only about 5 or 10 minutes of the talk will be devoted to shopping. Some cruise directors will guide you to certain shops, others will tell you where the main street is, how to get there, and when the stores open and close. Sometimes there are advertising brochures on a table by the door; these are provided by the shops themselves.

Many of the lines give handouts that you take with you that guide you around town and point out the best places for T-shirts.

There's just one catch to all this: The stores mentioned have paid to be mentioned. I'm not talking about kickbacks; I'm talking about what has become an accepted way of business these days—contracting an information service that the passenger believes to be an editorial service when in fact, it is an advertising service.

Of course, cruise directors, like all tour directors, are often offered kickbacks and freebies to persuade them to steer customers a certain way. Since everyone has been aware of these kickbacks for years, the port consultant method is now being employed to change the image.

Port lecturers are merely doing their jobs; they usually send you to the best stores in town simply because the best stores are the most successful and they have the most money and they can afford to hire these firms.

What happens here is that you aren't steered toward the small, the funky, the unknown, or the guy who simply hasn't paid up.

BEST BUY STRATEGIES

The best buys in any given port are items that are on sale or are promotional buys. No cruise director can keep track of these. It takes footwork—yours.

Some cruise directors and port lecturers are able to get discounts for their flock; such coupons are offered in handouts that the shop provides. Every 10% counts, so check it out.

MANY HAPPY RETURNS

I once made a videotape on shopping in the Caribbean for *Porthole Magazine,* and during part of it, I had to memorize and spit out legal spiel. Most of it was me doing my schtick, but one part was very important and so they had me memorize it. It dealt with "buyer's remorse," which I had never heard of, but which turns out to be a legal condition.

Now then, you hear a lot about how if you buy things in ship-recommended stores and something goes wrong, you can return them. This is a point that the cruise director and the port lecturer will make constantly, and you'll find it very reassuring. But they don't explain the legal fine print, or they'll mention it in passing, and you never even think, "huh?"

The guarantees do not include "buyer's remorse," which simply means you changed your mind. You woke up, you realized you overspent, you were stupid, you don't want it, or whatever, and the item is still brand new and perfect and never worn or used—but you can't return it.

Furthermore, the terms of the return when the item is faulty must meet the insurer's definitions, not your own personal appraiser's. Your jeweler at home says the ring is worth half what you paid for it, but the cruise ship and the store appraiser says, "Nope," the item is worth what you paid for it. No return, no refund. You lose.

If you have a problem with a store or with merchandise purchased there, take it to the cruise director, before you've left port (if this is possible). Most cruise lines guarantee merchandise, and you will be helped toward a refund or a repair.

PERFUME STRATEGIES
· ·

I have been trying to figure out the perfume business for years and have just gotten some of the basics straightened out. The stores in the Caribbean usually buy supplies from a distributor. While they may go to France for one reason or another, the system simply isn't set up for all of them to buy in France.

Normally, these retailers order stock from a Caribbean distributor or whichever branch of a big firm (the North American division, European division, or even Asian division) gives them the best deal— and yes, different branches of the same parent company try to undercut each other.

Stock in any given shop may come from Europe, the United States, Asia, or even South America. So it's very possible that the big-name French designer fragrance you are buying is made in Brazil under a license agreement. Or it's a French name made in the U.S. with essence shipped from France but mixed in a U.S. chemical plant. Does it smell the same? More or less. Does it react the same on your body? That's up for grabs—each body is different.

It's generally accepted that the French fragrance directly from France is the strongest and lasts the longest because of the type of alcohol that is used, which is organic. U.S. regulations require the use of denatured alcohol.

Now then, when a perfume shop owner in the Caribbean tells you that its prices are cheaper than in France, he's right: *His prices are less expensive than French retail prices. But* Americans never pay French retail prices anyway. What you really need to know is: Can you buy perfume in the Caribbean for more, less, or the same amount of money in Paris?

Here's the not-so-easy answer: It actually depends on the fragrance on a brand-by-brand basis!

The two best perfume shops in the Caribbean are **Roger Albert** in Martinique and **Tropicana** in St. Thomas. Roger Albert even gets new French fragrances before they are introduced in the U.S. Traditionally speaking, a French fragrance is introduced in September for Christmas selling or February or March for their version of Mother's Day (which is in May or June, the date moves each year) and then comes to the U.S. for Christmas of that same year, or for Christmas of the next year.

Distributors do not want the Caribbean to be undercutting American retailers on a new fragrance, so it will take another two months or so for a new scent to make it to Caribbean shelves.

Meanwhile, the official duty-free market, which the shops on your ship are a part of, are given perfume releases at different dates than regular retail.

Shopper's tip: Some items that are not available in Europe, whether at a discount or at full retail, are available in the Caribbean. This particularly means American-made, and probably licensed, products bearing a grand perfume's name.

About Caracas: If you want deals on perfume, you may want to buy your scent—and everyone else's—in Caracas, where the prices are so cheap they are embarrassing. (Would you believe $9 for a bottle of Shalimar?) There's only one catch. All the fragrance, cosmetics, and health/beauty aids here are "made in Venezuela." They're not illegal; they are licensed. The Shalimar smelled like real Shalimar, but it wasn't the same item I would have bought in Paris.

If you want real French fragrance, you should buy in Martinique or St. Martin, or from a reputable store on other islands—preferably in the Central, and not Southern, Caribbean.

Final tip: Some perfume shops are selling genuine imitation fragrances, or ones that smell similar to the grand perfumes but are cheaper (in price as well as quality). I don't mean fake, I mean a legal product created to smell like another fragrance. If you ask for perfume X and the store says, "We haven't got that, but we have one that smells just like it": BEWARE.

SHORE EXCURSION STRATEGIES

Shore excursions are terrific because they don't require you to think, which is possibly one of the reasons you picked the Caribbean. This is a vacation; you came to chill out. Many Caribbean excursions are water- and/or sport-related, some are even party boats so you leave your big ocean liner to get on a tiny pirate ship and get drunk. It's part of what the Caribbean is all about.

Others will want to tour an island, get to a big city, see several sights or even be taken to out-of-the-way places to experience the land and the people—the real people, not the ones standing around the pier.

While most shore excursions are well priced and try to offer good value for your money, you may want to figure costs on your own or try a day with a local guide or a taxi; if you go in with another couple (most cabs will fit four plus the driver), you will surely save money on shore excursion prices. Do, however, negotiate the price with a local driver, and make sure all financial matters are understood upfront. If you're going to rum factories, make sure you stress to your driver that you don't expect him to drink and drive.

Chapter Five

. . . .

DICTIONARY OF CARIBBEAN LIFE & STYLE

LIFE & STYLE

. . . .

For hundreds of years, both native populations and European colonists have enjoyed the weather and the relaxed lifestyle of the Caribbean Islands. In most cases, today's Caribbean lifestyle has evolved from this melting pot of specific colonial influences and native styles. Destinations that were once British colonies are different from ones that were or currently are associated with France.

Yet common to the region is the quality of the light that is reflected in the colors and the styles popular throughout almost every island. Many islands do have individual tastes, but there is an overarching Caribbean style that lives on—partially in your fantasies and partly in the colors and architecture associated with the climate.

Naturally, the climate influences not only the architecture but the cuisine, the clothing, the pace of life, and the original flavors that make us keep returning, year after year.

Allspice Common to several southern Caribbean Islands, this spice is created from unripe berries of the pimento tree (hold the olive, Mr. Bond). It tastes like a combination of cinnamon, nutmeg, and clove, and is sold on many islands at spice stands or in markets. The oil can be extracted and is used to treat upset stomachs; the spice can be ground and mushed into a plaster that is said to help relieve rheumatism.

Aloe   Known even in the U.S. for its healing properties, aloe is often sold in Caribbean markets. Use it to treat sunburn or mosquito bites.

Angostura Bitters   Angostura is actually the name of a city, reputedly a destination in Trinidad where a brew of distilled herbs and spices called Angostura Bitters was added to cocktails and is the key ingredient in a drink inappropriately called a Manhattan. (I mean, really—it was invented in Trinidad!)

   The original concoction was created several hundred years ago to treat upset tummies; despite the name, it is not bitter. The secret to the proper mixture of the bottled bitters is said to be guarded more closely than the recipe for Coca-Cola; only four men know how to brew the stew. You can visit the factory in Port of Spain, Trinidad, Monday through Friday, 9am to 1:30pm; $5 per person. Yes, of course they have a store on premises.

Anneaux Créole   Well, it's *les anneaux créoles,* to be proper about it. This French phrase refers to a type of gold, twisted hoop earring, made from molds that are known on sight by those who have learned to identify this art form—it just takes a trip to a jewelry store in Martinique or St. Martin. Sometimes these simple hoops are filled in with a filligree-like series of tiny golden balls (or Caribbean fruits) that have a pattern stamped on them, creating a lightweight beehive of golden dots.

Art   With all that light and all those colors, you can't help but attract artists—local and imported. There isn't as big a tradition in folk art as you might expect, although tin (see page 76) has made a place for itself as a folk-art form. Mostly you'll find paintings sold either as pieces of art, or reproduced on postcards, which depict either sea scenes or local scenes. I'm always drawn to market art, personally. Among those artists to check out while you travel:

- Mounette Radot (St. Martin): hot colors, local scenes, postcard reproductions available.
- Roland Richardson (St. Martin): colorful landscapes with broad strokes, almost Cezanne-like in some canvases. Oils, watercolors, hand-pulled etchings. This artist's name is Roland, but he's known locally as Vere.
- Miss Lassie (Grand Cayman): Lassie, Come Home! Sorry, her real name is Gladwyn Bush, and she is considered the local version of Grandma Moses. She is currently in her late 70s. Her style is dark yet vivid, naïve and spiritual; her paintings often are titled with Biblical quotations.
- Canute Calliste (Grenadines): Another 70-something artist with gallery and studio in cottage; expressionist naïve form discovered by *New York Times*. Collectors include former President George Bush.
- Amos Ferguson (Bahamas): Known as the Father of Bahamian Art, also in his late 70s, Ferguson's style is big and bold and clean with a naïve touch when in large scale. He was recently featured at the Smithsonian's Festival of American Folklife. His logo is scrawled "Paint by Mr. Amos Ferguson." A date follows; most works are titled as well.

Art Auctions at Sea   This is one of the most clever marketing ploys I've ever come across, but it does sort of scare me. Since cruise passengers are often captives (what a way to go), some marketing firms think those passengers can be sold anything. Many cruise lines now offer art auctions at sea, complete with gallery showings, color catalogs in your stateroom, and even televised (on the ship) proceedings. I would like to tell you that this art is going to become valuable, that these auctions offer sensational value, and that I shop this way all the time. I just can't. I would never buy art without knowing what it is and would much rather that you fell in love with something found locally on one of the islands that was woven with memories and meanings than something you perceived as a "good deal" offered on a cruise ship. That's just my opinion.

What's sold at these auctions is usually a lot of different styles by a lot of different artists at a variety of price points, to attract as wide a range of buyers as possible. There are prints, lithos, silk screens, and even works in oil; the people who run these auctions say that you can buy art at 50% less than its retail value by participating in one of these shipboard auctions. I happen to think that value in art (other than Van Gogh) is hard to nail down. Of course, if you love it, can afford it, and have to have it, by all means, go ahead and buy.

Bammy   Jamaican pancake made from cassava flour; served with soup or stew.

Banana   Yes, we have no education here. My darling photographer friend and British correspondent Ian Cook did not know that bananas grew upside down. See how broadening it is to travel around the world and get out of the grocery store . . . and the market!

Batik   Artistic process of dying fabric whereby designs are created on fabric in wax, and the fabric is dyed; the portions covered in wax do not absorb the dye. The more intricate the patterns and colors, the more sophisticated the batik. Rumored to be a Dutch method, this art form is often found in Indonesia and the Caribbean. The two most famous brands are **Caribelle** (worn by members of British Royal family—I know you really care) and **Java Wraps,** one of my personal faves. Tie dye is *not* batik.

Bay Rum   Distilled from leaves of our friend the pimento tree, another popular pan-Caribbean product used usually as an after-shave or pick-me-up skin tonic. *Do not drink!*

Black Coral Jewelry made from black coral is most often found in the Western Caribbean; the most famous designer and retailer is **Bernard Passman,** who sells in Grand Cayman, St. Thomas, and even Las Vegas. In most cases, the black coral is combined with gold. While there are sculptures and objets d'art, mostly the black and gold are worked together to form earrings, bracelets, rings, charms, cufflinks, and more.

Breadfruit Starchy vegetable, smooth on the outside, related to the durian of Asia. It is only edible when cooked and is served much like potatoes are.

Calabash Goodnight Mrs. Calabash, wherever you are; a Caribbean berry with a large husklike shell that is often dried and used as a cup or bowl.

Calling Station An enormous business has grown in phone-call connections between the Caribbean, the U.S., and Europe. All U.S. carriers have access lines, and some have direct-dial phones in port terminals; but a different twist is the sale of phone cards that are then used in various Calling Stations dotted around the islands (several kiosks sell them at the San Juan terminals alone). The phone rates with these cards are much, much lower. However, I haven't tested any of these systems.

Note that most of these Calling Stations (whether named that or something else) also offer fax services. Faxing from a ship usually costs about $15 a minute (satellite time is expensive), so using a land-based office is a good idea.

Carnival I am not talking about the cruise line.

Carnival is traditionally the season of revelry that ends with Mardi Gras (Fat Tuesday)—the day before Ash Wednesday, which is the first day of Lent (a period of going without in order to remember Christ's suffering). Lent ends after 40 days with Easter. Mardi Gras dates change from year to year, since Easter isn't on a set day.

From New Orleans to Rio, Carnival is big business in the winter months; each community throws colorful and sometimes exotic events designed to generate business and photo ops. It's become a high-season winter tradition, usually in February, on most Caribbean Islands. In truth, it has little religious significance, but it's a lot of fun! In order to distance themselves from the original religious significance, and to carry on as a tourist attraction, many islands have renamed Carnival with a local phrase. There's always plenty to buy to help the celebrations—or the sell-abrations.

Cassava   A starchy root vegetable also known as manioc. It's always served cooked—it must be processed (boiled, soaked, and fermented), since in raw form, wild cassava is poisonous. Tapioca is made from cassava.

CBI   The Caribbean Basin Initiative was passed in 1983 to create economic growth in the Caribbean. This law allows factories to create ready-to-wear products sold in the U.S. and for looser duty-free laws for tourists.

Chattel House   Tiny, wood-frame house that fits neatly on a concrete slab so that it becomes portable; usually painted bright colors and often trimmed with gingerbread.

Cigars   Possibly the single hottest item for sale in the Caribbean are cigars—especially Cuban cigars, which can legally be smoked in the Caribbean Basin but cannot legally be brought into the U.S. Cigar smoking is definitely on a roll these days; most ships now have a Smoking Room or a Smokers Night, or sometimes an event each night at sea. These events are mostly attended by men, but some women usually also come to smoke cigars. After all, a woman is a woman, but a cigar is a smoke.

Many politicans have called for a review of the 1960 laws of embargo against Cuba, so it's possible that someday you'll be able to bring Cuban cigars into the U.S. legally. Either way, there's a lot to learn. Vintage cigars—a specialty part of the business—

are 20 years old or older. Stocks of pre-Castro era cigars do come on the market every now and then and are usually sold at auction, often in London. I don't think I'd trust any Caribbean "pre-Castros."

There's so much to learn in fact, that you may want to buy a book on the subject, or start with an issue (or subscription) of *Cigar Aficionado* magazine, available on most newsstands in the U.S. and sometimes in Europe and the Caribbean at luxury hotels or at cigar shops.

Certainly, if you're a beginner, you should learn the famous names and do some experimenting before you start buying the big name cigars (which can be as much as $15 each). Cigars are as sophisticated as fine wines, and there are many levels of expertise. Also note that there is an enormous business in fake Cuban cigars, which is a very shrewd crime, because once you have illegally smuggled them back into the U.S., you can't report that your money has gone up in smoke, so to speak. Fine cigars are very expensive; only buy them from a reputable dealer, and avoid buying into any deals that are too good to be true—especially in the Western Caribbean, where the fake business is rife.

I'm in love with many of the matchboxes and cigar boxes, which have fabulous old labels and graphic arts. The matches are given away just about everywhere; I found one nice guy in Antiqua who was willing to give me—as a gift just for the asking—several empty cigar boxes. These were the treasure of the trip; great for crafts projects or packing other gifts from the area. It is not illegal to bring empty Cuban cigar boxes into the U.S.

Okay, here are a few tips to get you started:

- It's considered bad form to leave the cigar band on the smoke when you light up. This is like showing off a designer logo—tacky, tacky. Do be sophisticated about this; you place the band in an ashtray but don't scrunch it up, so that everyone can still see the label. It is considered very "American" (read *gauche*) to leave the band on while smoking.

- A cigar must be cut before you can light it, there ain't no draw if you don't cut it! While I'm sure you've seen movies wherein someone bites off the end of the cigar, there are tools to perform this surgery.

- Proper long wooden matches are correct for lighting cigars. You don't need a fancy lighter, but you do need the right matches. The cigar is lighted from the tip of the flame, not the center. Roll and puff as you light up until the entire cigar is properly lit, then take it out of your mouth and moan with pleasure. Okay, the moaning is optional.

- At the end of your smoke, do not snub out the cigar, just lay it in the ashtray and let it fade out and die. You can relight a cigar if you haven't finished it; there are tubes for storing partially smoked smokes.

- Cigar smoking is best considered as an after-dinner sport, so that your taste buds have already enjoyed the fine cuisine of the chef and the wine you chose with your meal. Since some people object to cigar smoke (although fine cigars do not smell bad), private smokes are usually held around 10pm, after the dinner hour but early enough to still enjoy a good smoke and perhaps good conversation.

- I smoked cigars when I was 21 and was only a little bit affected; I buy a good cigar every now and then and always return to the same friends— you can trust an Upmann Corona; Cohiba Siglo V, or Partagas Lusitania. Actually all three of these houses (Upmann, Cohiba, Partagas) can be trusted in any type of roll; they are all expensive and should cost about $15. Note that Upmann relocated to the Dominican Republic after the Cuban Revolution, so there are two Upmanns;

the one that is legally doing business in the U.S. is also known as Consolidated Cigar Corporation.

Conch All I'll say is that it's pronounced "konk." I caught one when I was 11 and was quite distressed to find that there was someone living inside that gorgeous shell I wanted as a souvenir, and I was expected to eat that critter for dinner.

Crop Over Summer festival held in Barbados to create Carnival-like atmosphere out of season. Traditionally celebrates the end of the sugarcane season and harvest.

Curaçao Aside from being the name of an island, it is also the name of an orange liqueur.

Dreadlocks Hey, lighten up, mon! We call 'em dreads—those long ringlets of quasi-braided, twisted, knotted hair. Don't be surprised if every otherwise sane female in the family suddenly wants corn-plaits (rows of tiny braids) or dreads while visiting the Basin; beach vendors and TT (tourist trap) owners will comply, although asking prices are often very high. It takes a few hours to do the whole head and will often cost $150 to $200. With some bargaining, you can sometimes get a partial "do" for $50. Fake dreads can also be bought and woven in if hair is not long enough for the full effect.

Duty Free Destination that does not levy import duties or tariffs on goods from other countries; these goods are then resold to the public, usually without additional local taxation.

Flying Fish Small fish that leap out of the waves while moving fins, thus appearing to fly—a local delicacy in southern Caribbean Islands, especially Barbados. Sometimes refered to as "fly fish." They don't really fly but they sure do fry.

Goombay Bahamas word that refers to the rhythm of drums; has been adapted to the name of a festival.

Eddy Grant   Singer/producer who is to current calypso what Harry Belafonte was to my childhood. His Barbados-based label is called Ice Records. His newest sound is called ring-bang. Could I make this up? Day-o no, mon!

Green Turtle   Farmed in the Caymans for the hide. You can take on-shore excursion tours to turtle farms, most of which have shops on premises.

Guavaberry   National fruit of St. Martin; although guavaberry jam is a more traditional presentation, it's often made into a liqueur (combined with rum) and sold. Also known as a traditional Christmas drink in the islands.

Haitian Art   Very specific type of naïve-style painting sold throughout the Caribbean. While painting is the primary art form, a unique style of silhouette tinwork, usually with pegs or hooks and painted in bright colors, is also in evidence. The style comes from Haiti but is sold all over, since Haiti is mostly closed to tourists.

Higgler   Jamaican term, specific to women at one time, referring to stall holders and vendors in a market.

Hurricane   A wind of 64 knots and over, but more likely to reach 150 to 175 knots. Hurricane season is technically between July and November, though September and October are the worst months. Often by August those winds can change the course of your off-seasonably priced vacation.

Jerk   A spice combination made popular in Jamaica, but now widespread throughout the Caribbean. Jerk sauces come in homemade and branded versions; naturally, my favorite brand is called Suzy's.

Jug-Jug   Barbados's version of haggis. Don't ask.

Junkanoo   Bahama Carnival-like festival that actually begins in December (on Boxing Day, the day after Christmas).

Limbo Cruise ship, Caribbean, and Bar Mitzvah ritual dance during which sane people ask themselves just how *low* they can go.

Luciano In the Caribbean, it ain't Pavoratti. He's a hot Jamaican reggae star.

Mahogany Type of hardwood from trees grown in the rain forest and tropical Caribbean; it's now considered endangered and especially collectible. Colonial Caribbean furniture (and most genuine early American Colonial furniture) is made of mahogany.

Salad bowls and small decorative items are still made and sold in some islands. Because several tropical trees have wood that looks like mahogany, new items are most likely made from this rather than from the *S. mahogani* tree.

Mango Tropical fruit of Asia also grown in the Caribbean; in season, you'll get 15 mangoes for $1 in Barbados. There are over 500 varieties, so expect the fruit to look different than what you're used to at home. Prices often vary, especially for tourists.

To best tackle ye olde slippery mango: slice the mango on each side of the central pit. Toss the pit and the central fruit—sorry; I know this is wasteful, but I am teaching you the easiest as well as the neatest method. Okay, you now have two separate ovals of mango. Slice into the fruit between the skin and the fruit, making a deep and complete circle around each oval. Score the mango diagonally in each direction. Now turn the mango skin inside out so that the mango bits pop up and the oval is now convex. Slice off bits and enjoy.

Bob Marley The legend lives on. This reggae king died of cancer in Miami in 1981. Son Ziggy and his band, the Melody Makers, have continued the family music tradition. The beat goes on.

Mola Multilayer, reverse appliqué fabric art form made by Cuna Indians from the San Blas Islands. It is sold there and in the Mexican Caribbean.

Nutmeg   Not to be confused with allspice, nutmeg is most often found on Grenada, although several islands in the Southern Caribbean claim to be spice islands. Now then, for you overgrown hippies, don't ingest nutmegs—two of 'em can kill you and more than half a teaspoon is hallucinogenic. Just a sprinkle will do the trick.

Off-shore   Banking term for financial transactions often conducted through Caribbean-based banks (most often in the Cayman Islands or the Bahamas). Funds funneled through these channels can be governed and taxed by laws possibly more favorable than those in the U.S. and U.K.

Pan   Part of the steel band, not part of Julia Child's kitchen collection—there's a tenor pan and a base pan. When the guys get together to rehearse, they "beat pan."

Pareo   See *sarong.*

Piece of Eight   Swashbuckling expression that I associate with pirates and often see in jewelry or in jewelry ads. It seems that back then a gold piece was worth exactly eight Spanish *reals,* and was thus stamped with the number 8. Large business in fakes; be careful.

Plantain   Tropical cooking banana also made into baked chips and sold as a snack food like potato chips. Again, never eaten raw! Tons o' vendors in Old San Juan sell these chips in the streets near the cruise terminal.

Rum (By Gum)   Columbus brought sugarcane with him to the islands on his second trip (1493), and the crop has been thriving ever since. Sugarcane is distilled and then mixed with a few other ingredients to make it more palatable. Those ingredients, whether oranges, sea water, or tamarinds, account for the different flavors of rum and explain why there are so many different brands, and how they all seem to thrive.

Some rums are aged for up to 15 years, some are doubly distilled, others get their different flavor from the wood casks in which they are aged. French rums are usually made from sugarcane juice rather than molasses. The rums of Jamaica, Haiti, Martinique, and Barbados are considered the heavy rums, while those made in Puerto Rico and the Virgin Islands are drier and lighter.

Flavored rums are a rather new development, but look for coconut rum, mango rum, or spiced rum as some of the exotics.

Barbados is the most famous rum island; the best known brand is **Mount Gay**. Not only can you buy the rum, but there are T-shirts with the bottle's label on them; these are considered prime gifts. Rum factories on the island of Barbados date back to 1647.

Yet others will tell you that nothing beats Jamaican rum; the two most famous brands are **Appleton** and **Sangster's**. Tours of both factories are available or can be arranged by **The Touring Society of Jamaica in Ocho Rios** (☎ 809/974-5831; fax 809/974-5830). If you just want the buzz but don't want to dance, try **Wray & Nephew's** "white overproof" rum at 126 proof, or 63% alcohol.

Bacardi, from Puerto Rico, sells the most rum in the United States and has a factory tour (just outside of San Juan) as a tourist highlight.

If your taste in factory outlets runs toward the drinkable, here's an assortment of distilleries that have visitor centers (tasting rooms) and/or tours; most tours are free, and samples are given to those of legal drinking age. Distilleries are open all year round, except for Sundays and holidays. Bacardi, Puerto Rico; Appleton, Jamaica; Cruzan, St. Croix; Mount Gay, Barbados; St. James, Martinique.

Sarong   Popular way of dressing up a bathing suit on board ship or in public in the Caribbean; large scarf tied artfully at the hips to cover lower portion of body, also known as a *pareo*.

Sea Island Cotton   I thought this was from the Carolinas, but this type of cotton is also grown in the West Indies.

Spanish Main   Another of my favorite pirate terms. This is the coastal region of South America from Panama to the Orinoco River delta, which happens to have quite a few cruise ports and Caribbean destinations along it. So, now you can plunder it.

Steel Band   Band made up of instruments created from steel drums from local oil refineries.

Sugarcane   Principal crop of many Caribbean Islands, responsible for production of rum and therefore related directly to the terrible Triangle Trade: Slaves were brought from Africa to plantations in the Caribbean to work the cane fields, the rum (and sugar) were brought to Boston where cash changed hands, and the ships returned again to Africa to repeat the triangle.

Tequila   Mexican blend of blue agave sugars, which are cut and mixed with other sugars and fermented, then double distilled and aged. How long the booze stays in the oak to age is written in the name of the brew; *anejo* (old) must stay in the barrel at least 1 year. There are gourmet tequilas; **Don Julio** is one of the smoother blends.

Vanilla   Sold in Mexican Caribbean ports in much stronger form than in the U.S.—yes, dear, it's got a high alcohol content.

Voodoo   Black magic.

Whim Plantation   St. Croix plantation–turned–museum known for its colonial antiques, which are now reproduced through **Baker Furniture's Milling Road** division. Also famous as the site of an annual antiques flea market, held in March, considered the best in the Caribbean.

Chapter Six

· · · · · · ·

SOUTH FLORIDA

THE PORTS OF MIAMI & FT. LAUDERDALE
· ·

The true gateway to the Caribbean is still Florida.
Most cruise ships leave from Miami or Ft. Lauderdale; most island-bound flights are routed through
Miami, although several hub cities around America
can serve as the jumping off point for a flight to
San Juan. While yes, some ships now depart directly
from San Juan, or from an island port, *most* ships
still use either the Port of Miami or Port Everglades
in Ft. Lauderdale.

The cruise business is enormously important to
south Florida; both cities have immaculate port terminals, though the one in Ft. Lauderdale is more
isolated. Miami's port is just about in downtown
Miami and feels like it's part of the energy of the
downtown harbor space, whereas Ft. Lauderdale is
just sort of out there with the palm trees and the
deep blue sea. Never mind; **The Galleria,** which is
the biggest mall in the area, sends a free shuttle bus
to the port in Ft. Lauderdale.

While Miami and Ft. Lauderdale are not very
far apart, and sometimes people interchange the airports for easier connections or getaways, there's
more than 1 hour of transportation time between
them, so few visitors take in both destinations.

MIAMI

. . . .

Miami's debut on the social scene is way past the days of *Miami Vice*; these days Madonna and Gianni Versace are very much part of the South Beach scene. Miami even has its own music, its own kind of clothing, and its own destinational feel. There's been so much said about the area recently that, despite the hype, you feel you just have to make South Beach part of your what's-it-all-about Caribbean visit. South Beach isn't the whole of Miami, but for a 1-day visit, it's something you'll probably want to see.

While cruisers may just get to spend a day or two in Miami, the point indeed is that you do try to stay and have at least one evening to fully take in South Beach. Don't arrive in the morning; enroute to your ship, visit **Bayside Marketplace** (the big downtown festival mall) and feel that you've done south Florida.

If you don't plan to soak up the Latin beat, to see what South Beach really means, to feel the feel of the colors and the weather and the cultural dance, well then, at least plan your visit to do some comparison shopping. Miami just might have better bargains than some of the islands you will visit!

ARRIVING IN MIAMI

. . . .

If your ship departs from the Port of Miami, you'll undoubtedly fly into Miami International Airport. You will be met by representatives of your cruise line, who will help identify your luggage and make sure it gets on your bus. Chances are you won't see your luggage again until it's in your stateroom, so after you make sure the cruise people have it, you won't really have to worry about it. You should have already placed the proper luggage tags on your bags so they can be taken directly to your stateroom.

GETTING AROUND
· ·

Usually it's easier (and cheaper) to accept the free transfer from the airport to the port and then take a taxi to your day-trip destinations, since the Port of Miami is not very far from downtown or Miami Beach.

If you have arrived prior to your cruise departure, you can rent a car at the airport or transfer directly to your hotel. On the day of departure, the cruise company usually sends a bus to the hotels on their land-package programs to transfer passengers and their luggage. If you're not on the ship's package, you may be able to buy a transfer from the hotel to the ship, provided the ship services your chosen hotel or provided you can get yourself (and your things) to a hotel they do service.

You can always taxi to the port on your own. Taxis cost about $20 from the airport to the port.

Do note that just as in the hotel business, there is a "check in" time, and your ship will not be ready for boarding before this time period. This means that you may indeed have a layover in Miami—and it's just too good a place to miss. So send your luggage on its way, grab your sunglasses and a hat, and yes, sunblock too, and get out of that vacation mentality. Save that for *mañana;* today is Miami, and Miami is hopping.

If you have tons of time on your hands and you like this kind of thing, send your luggage directly from the airport to the ship and then hop on a Metrobus—Miami has pretty good public transportation for the pier and downtown (but not for the 'burbs). The bus can get you to the port, downtown, Miami Beach, or anyplace else for about $1.50 per person. You can even connect to MetroMover, which is an elevated tram that circles downtown and will give you a good overview of the area and maybe even the ships in the bay.

Of course, if you want to go shopping, get off the bus.

LANDLUBBER'S DELIGHT

. . . .

Miami is not lacking in gorgeous hotels or package deals to lure you to the city; most cruise lines offer "turnaround" packages that enable you to transfer to a hotel property for 1, 2, or 3 days either prior to your cruise or immediately after.

I've done my own exploring; the hotels I've chosen for you offer opportunities to combine shopping with either location, convenience, or simple south Florida "being there." If you haven't been to Miami recently, believe me, this city is something quite different than the rest of America. It deserves your attention.

DELANO
1685 Collins Ave., Miami Beach.
☎ *800/555-5001 in the U.S., or 305/672-2000.*

I went to the Delano to look, because I had to go, because I was curious. I felt jaded and was not inclined to be impressed, so when I say, "boy oh boy," well guys, trust me on this one—once before you die, you have to at least walk through the lobby. It'd be better if you stayed a few days, or at least a full day, and got to use the spa, have a few meals, and hang, but even if you just wander in, this is a real treat. Doubles go for $295–$395 in high season and drop to $200–$300 in the off-season. I came for breakfast, which is an affordable way to be part of the whole scene. (You can dine outside or inside.) The lobby is dramatically amazing. The health club spa (called Aqua) is owned separately and does take day-trippers. You simply haven't been to Florida if you don't organize your trip to spend some time here. Oh yes, they even have a sensational gift shop! The rooms aren't always heaven, and the bathrooms aren't the best in the business, but the hotel is one big scene. Calvin Klein anyone?

🛍 **CAVALIER**
1320 Ocean Dr., South Beach. ☎ *800/688-7678
or 305/531-8800.*

This is my personal find, and while it's not for everyone, it is a treasure. The hotel is one of the deco
rehabs you've been reading about; it's got a young
clientele and it can get noisy, especially on weekends. The people are not the type you'll see on your
cruise ship or in the lobby of the Delano or the
Fountainebleau, but the rates are incredibly low
(from $145 in high season, from $95 other times),
the people who work here could not be nicer and
you are right smack in the middle of the scene.
Decor is Jamaican deco flash—they even have
Caribbean-flavored bath amenities. The hotel places
you inside the picture—not on the outside, looking
in. There are just fewer than 50 rooms, so book
ahead or grab the sister hotel next door, the **Leslie**.
Be sure to eat breakfast at the Leslie, since there is
no restaurant in the Cavalier and the two hotels are
related in style.

SHERATON BAL HARBOUR
9701 Collins Ave., Bal Harbour.
☎ *800/284-2000 or 305/865-7511.*

Directly across from one of the most prestigious
shopping centers in the United States (the **Bal
Harbour Stores**), the Sheraton is one of those new,
glamorous ones, more like a spa than an old-
fashioned Miami waterfront hotel. It's not in
Miami Beach or South Beach, but just a little bit
north, not far away. Rooms start at $220 in high
season, $130 in the off-season.

The bad news is that location-wise you're in
no-man's land and need a taxi to get to the scene—
but that's not hard, especially if you're just heading
out for an evening in South Beach. Comfortable,
easy, do-able and safe. The good news is that you
can almost spend the night at Neiman-Marcus.

MIAMI INTERNATIONAL AIRPORT HOTEL
Concourse E. ☎ *800/327-1276 or 305/
871-4100.*

Don't laugh—knowing about this hotel has been a
godsend. If you think of all the times that New
England airports close and visitors (like me) are
stranded, then you'll appreciate that this airport has
a great hotel and the hotel is *inside* the airport—not
on a ring road or adjacent to a nearby highway.

Ideal for travelers or cruisers who must make
inconvenient connections and still get a good night's
sleep, this hotel is nicer than many resorts we've
visited in the Caribbean. Prices are moderate—about
$150 per night for a double—and you're smack in
the middle of the giant airport shopping mall.

A porter will take your luggage to your airline
and will carry your liquor for you. You can take
public transportation to other sights or shopping
opportunities, or just go wild in the plethora of airport stores. If you think I'm nuts, just remember
this listing when you get stuck or stranded and I
promise you, this is a find.

MIAMI NEIGHBORHOODS

. . . .

Miami is a large city with a diverse population
and suburbs that basically stretch all the way past
Ft. Lauderdale and into different area codes. If you
come as a snowbird you may learn all these areas,
but cruise passengers need to know only a sprin-
kling of directions—just enough to know the
must-do, must-see areas and to not get South Beach
confused with Miami Beach!

Bayside Bayside Harbour Market isn't really a
mall, it's a happening. Created by The Rouse Corporation (those retail developers who gave us Faneuil
Marketplace in Boston and Harborplace in Balti-
more), Bayside is a two-pronged, two-tiered shopping, eating, and socializing community right on
the waterfront of downtown Miami. This is what's

known as festival shopping, and few locals even shop here—the place was seemingly created for tourists and day-trippers who come and go with the cruise ships parked in the harbor around the corner.

Flags wave in the breeze; summer colors cover the stucco, the wood, and the rails. But the best part is that the mix of retailers is so original. The standard chain stores have not gobbled up all the space, so that while you find a few of the names you'd expect (The Limited, Ann Taylor), there are also stands and shops and pushcarts and vendors you've never heard of. There's also that perfect combination of stores that seem right for the area—such as **Landau,** which sells fake diamonds and copies of Bulgari gems, and **H_2O Plus,** which is found in a number of malls, but not in so many malls as to be common. H_2O Plus is one of my favorite sources for bath and beauty treatments because quality is high and price is moderate; it seems altogether fitting that they have a shop right there at the "H_2O-front" in Miami. If your stateroom has a bathtub, you might want to spring for some of the bath treatments or suds as a splurge; if not, consider some of the massage oils if you are thinking of a little romance on the high seas.

The regular giants of retailing are also present, including the **Disney Store, The Gap, Victoria's Secret,** and more. You'll taste Caribbean and Cuban flavors as they appear in south Florida at the upstairs Food Court. There's also a great bar at the far end with a mighty powerful singles scene.

Part of what makes Bayside sing, besides the weather and the energy created by the flags and the architecture and the very design of the place, is this mix of regular retail with the pushcarts and vendor stalls; it creates an almost fleamarket-like ambience. A lot of them sell junk, but there's something so merry about the atmosphere that you almost feel compelled to check out the junk, as if it just might be the best junk you'll see on your trip.

There are designer fakes, in terms of leather goods, sold right there, and all sorts of copies and inspirations and things. One of the vendors just sells silly telephones; I bought my husband one that is a baseball. And according to the owner of the stall, these phones will work in any country.

Bayside is open 7 days a week, Monday to Thursday, 10am to 10pm; Friday to Saturday, 10am to 11pm; Sunday 11am to 9pm. The mall is safe at all hours, but don't go wandering around the nearby streets, even across the avenue, at night or alone.

Downtown   Bayside is separated from the downtown shopping area by a loop-de-loop exit ramp off of Interstate 95; and while it's only a block or two away, this wide thoroughfare that leads onto a highway makes it seem farther than it really is.

Flagler Street is the core of the downtown district; it is busy during the week with visitors from South America and the islands and with people who work in nearby office towers. Weekends are pretty dead, but stores are still open (even on Sunday), so if this is the best you can do, you can get some basic shopping done here. If you crave a discounter such as **Marshall's** or **Ross Dress for Less,** this is the place.

I can't tell you this is a great shopping area, or to stroll till you're too pooped to shop another inch, but there are two discounters right here (see page 95).

A few blocks away there's a small **Burdine's** department store, and adjacent to that is North Miami Avenue, where there are a lot of fabric shops. I mention this because I can never find resources like these at home, and even in New York City, things are much more expensive. They just have great and sometimes inexpensive fabrics here. If you sew, you may want to spend an hour or so looking around. I say sometimes inexpensive because some of the stores carry top-of-the-line European fabrics as well as junk; some are all junk. I have found gauzy things, flocked velvets, chiffons, all sorts of things that I could never find in New York. I start by going directly to **SNA Fabrics Centennial Textile Corporation,** 31 North Miami Avenue, which has designer fabrics and everything else. Be prepared to stay at least an hour if you love this sort of thing. After your visit here, explore the one-block area with other stores for the full effect, although this is by far the best store of the bunch.

Bal Harbour The minute you walk up (if you bus) or pull up (if you drive) to Bal Harbour you know it will be special—there's a posh feeling to the density of the jungle of plantings so that you know you are stepping into paradise. The shopping center is not a covered mall but a plaza with a center garden; there are two levels with a hundred shops, including anchors at either end: **Neiman-Marcus** and **Saks Fifth Avenue.**

Along the way, there's **Celine, Ralph Lauren/ Polo, Hermès,** and more.

Don't forget the bookstores, as paperbacks will be expensive on your trip. This is a good stop for pricing items before you start your Caribbean vacation. If something is on sale, buy it in the United States. Tourneau is one of the world's leading watch shops—price them if you are planning on buying a watch in the Caribbean, and be sure to get the warranty information. The warranty may be worth a lot of money.

South Beach The tip of Miami Beach is called South Beach, now sometimes written as (but hardly ever called) SoBe. This is also called the Deco District by some; it's the area where much of the art deco architecture of the 1930s has be rehabbed and where color and style and cruisers (all kinds) have gone hog-wild.

While it continues to evolve and come of age, it is really a night happening and a scene. It isn't about shopping, it's about bodies and sex and seeing and being seen. Even if you're just observing, it's something to behold. By no means should you get South Beach mixed up with Miami Beach (see below).

South Beach has a few very original retailers which are hot and exciting and out of the ordinary, although I get a lot of people asking me for finds all the time and I have to confess to them that there are always more stores but there are very few really good ones that I would call finds. There are beach shops, mainstream chains that are in cute rehabs, and a few hot spots, which I have listed in the "Miami Resources" section (see page 92).

By the way, as a simple trick for getting around any place in Miami Beach: The streets work on a grid system with the numbering so that 800 Ocean Drive is at Eighth Street, etc. This only works on oceanfront areas, but it's an easy way to get found or to work your way from store to store.

Miami Beach South Beach happens pretty much along Ocean Drive, Collins Avenue, Washington Street, and, most importantly, Lincoln Road. Miami Beach begins around 15th Street, where SoBe ends and Collins Avenue sort of deadends for a block. Miami Beach is actually, especially for the shopper, an inland kind of thing.

Sure, you've got your Fountainebleau thing here, you've got your upper Collins Avenue beginning around 23rd Street and continuing into the 70s or so, but the heart of the neighborhood is actually the **Lincoln Road Mall,** which is downtown Miami Beach re-created as a pedestrian area for shoppers, strollers, and people who are too old to think SoBe is cute or funny. It is not an enclosed mall!

My favorite restaurant in Miami, **Pacific Time,** is here—and there are some interesting shops (namely **Browne's!!!**), but this area is also most fun in the evening—stores stay open until 10pm or later. The feel is much more middle class than South Beach, and may be more your glass of iced tea. It can be sad in daylight, although more and more retailers are taking advantage of the fact that there's so much space and continue to move in to jazz things up. This area will eventually sizzle . . . or flop.

The idea has been to fill it with antique shops and vintage clothing hangouts and coffeehouses and art galleries, and while there is some of that, as well as a fabulous mosaic water fountain made of broken bits of dishes, the area is not coming together as quickly as I would like it to. The newish **Aveda** shop (no. 932) is the epitome of everything this area is meant to be, yet there aren't as many of these "Oh, wow!" stores as I want there to be.

When the most exciting part of the stroll is to stand outside the ballet studio and watch little girls take their lessons, then you know there's charm but not a lot of action!

REAL PEOPLE NEEDS

There are drugstores and mini-marts everywhere in South Beach; I usually stop by Compass market, 860 Ocean Drive, because it has everything you could need. It's very much a part of the scene, so while you're buying sunglasses, juice, bottled water, magazines, and rum punch, you can stare at everyone else. They also have a business center so you can send a fax or mail a package. Open 7 days a week.

SNACK & SHOP

PACIFIC TIME
915 Lincoln Road Mall, Miami Beach.
☎ *305/534-5979.*

How can I love a restaurant in Miami Beach because it's so New York–LA–big-city chic? Don't miss it if you care. In fact, if you really care, reserve ahead.

SOUTH BEACH BRASSERIE
910 Lincoln Road Mall, Miami Beach.
☎ *305/534-5511.*

Okay, so I'd follow Michael Caine anywhere. Book in advance. Langan's goes Miami Mediterraneé, both in cuisine and decor.

THE NEWS CAFÉ
800 Ocean Dr., South Beach. ☎ 305/531-0392.

Eat inside or out, have drinks, read, stare. You haven't been to South Beach if you don't stop by. Right on the ocean, right in the heart of the scene, right easy on the wallet. Simply right on.

MIAMI RESOURCES
. . . .
Beachwear

There are stores that sell beachwear, bathing suits, and even surfer looks just about everywhere, especially in SoBe, along the Lincoln Road Mall, and in main tourist areas like Bayside.

AQUA
650 Lincoln Road Mall, Miami Beach.

Swimwear by Blueman.

BEACH HOUSE
Bal Harbour Shops, 9700 Collins Ave.,
Miami Beach.

This is not for the person who possibly forgot a bathing suit or wants to add on one more before the cruise. This is a chic, fancy, expensive resource for the best in body and beachwear, including La Perla and Gottex.

2 THE EXTREME
700 Lincoln Road Mall, Miami Beach.

I am way too old for this—bike clothes from a rap star . . . hmmm, well, you had to know. There are bikes, helmets, clothes, bike parts, and everything hot and hip and bright and beachy. A little beach music, please.

Beauty & Bath

AVEDA
932 Lincoln Road Mall, Miami Beach.

This is the perfect rehab, the perfect introduction to everything Miami and the Deco District should be. Located on the Lincoln Road Mall, this branch of the famous aromatherapy treatment house is in what should be a landmark building that has been redone in high-tech deco style. Tea is served in the rear—that's herbal tea, my dear, not high tea (and it's free, this is the South, remember?). They even offer the hair color shampoo and conditioner system that is great for sunworshipers because it keeps hair colors from fading in the sun or in harshly treated chemical-laden water. There's another shop in Palm Beach, of course.

BROWNE'S & CO. APOTHECARY
841 Lincoln Road Mall, Miami Beach.

I'm not certain what's best about this store—the fact that it's large and well stocked with the best of European and designer bath and beauty lines; that they have tons of brochures and information on all the lines; that they are open at night; or that they are next door to Pacific Time, one of my favorite restaurants. Your Miami experience will be complete when you do some evening shopping on the mall and take in this store for soaps, aromatherapy, shampoos, cures, Shu Uemura makeup, French drugstore and dime-store brands, and more. They have mail order via a toll-free phone. One of the best stores in America, honest.

HANNA & HER SCISSORS
541 Lincoln Road Mall, Miami Beach.

I can't tell you that I've used this beauty salon, but I love the name! It's simple but chic enough to be trusted—from the looks of it, down home and you can probably walk in off the street.

Big Names

Most of the big-name international designers are in the Bal Harbour Shops, a mall at the northern end of Miami Beach. South Beach has quite a few free-standing designer shops, all done to match the local deco style—check out everyone from **Armani A/X** to **Versace** with **Banana Republic, Benetton,** and **The Gap** in the middle. Most of the stores are grouped around 8th Street on either Collins Avenue or Washington Avenue. Check out also **ABS, Betsey Johnson, Kenneth Cole, Express, Danskin, Todd Oldham,** and **The Body Shop.** Most of these stores don't open before 11am.

Books

NEWS CAFÉ
800 Ocean Dr., South Beach.

Cutting edge is the word here, from postcards to books to cigars to magazines to diners—buy beach books or books on local style. See and be seen. Best postcards in Miami.

Cigars

CIGAR COLLECTION
534 Lincoln Road Mall, Miami Beach.

Since everyone in the world seems to have gone cigar crazy lately, this shop will tickle your funny bone, even if you don't smoke. That's because there's a man who sits in the window and rolls cigars; you could watch all day.

News Café
800 Ocean Dr., South Beach.

They sell far more than cigars, but if you crave a smoke, stop in for the scene of your life (see above).

Costume Jewelry

Landau
Bayside Marketplace, 400 Biscayne Blvd., Miami.

Often when I am in Miami, I realize that I am totally unprepared for what passes as fashion there, and that I have not brought along enough glitz. Since you may indeed need your diamonds or your Bulgari look-alikes on your cruise, you can pop in here for excellent quality costume jewelry. This is the firm that used to own the Ciro and Ken Lane brands and still has some of the lines; they also have a wide range of prices, beginning around $25. They make a good quality fake but be sure of what you want because there are no refunds.

Department Stores

Burdines
22 E. Flagler St., Miami.

I don't care how excited you are, this Burdines is so boring it will put you to sleep.

Discounters

If you've forgotten something for the cruise or think you might want to expand your wardrobe, now is the time to do so, as prices in Florida are more reasonable than in the islands. South Florida has a bigger selection and downtown Miami has discounters—old-fashioned American discounters (even if the signs are in Spanish) like the ones you have at home, like **Marshalls** and **Ross Dress for Less**.

MARSHALL'S
International Galleria, Flagler Ave., Miami.

Do I hear a waltz? Just what every visitor to a tourist place needs, a non-touristy discount store for last-minute, real people needs. Yes!

ROSS DRESS FOR LESS
100 S. Biscayne Blvd., downtown.

Head up the escalators to get to this modern, and rather new, downtown discount store. The signs are all in English and Spanish; the store carries clothing for men, women, and children, as well as perfume, gift items, home goods, and a little of everything else. If you might need something for the trip but don't want to spend much, this is the place to visit. Across the street from the *Challenger* monument.

EXIT SHOPS CLEARANCE CENTER
2700 Biscayne Blvd., Miami.

Exit Shops has a big reputation with local ladies who buy much of their resort, weekend, and work clothing here. This small chain of stores weaves some European designer stock into their own version of the local look. That means that, to my eye, most of the styles are very Florida. There are regular retail stores in all the right addresses (such as Boca Raton and the Bal Harbour Shops), but there is an "outlet" shop, where the leftovers go to die, right downtown, not far from Bayside. Most items are 50% to 75% off; a code system is used, so read the signs and don't go by the price tags. Park in the rear. I saw some beige Emanuel Ungaro suits that were nice (same prices as Loehmann's) but I wasn't knocked out. Still, this kind of shopping is always hit or miss. New stock is added daily; hours are unusual: Monday to Friday, 11am to 5pm; no weekend hours.

Home Style

NU-D-ZINE
1006 Lincoln Road Mall, Miami Beach.

Despite the weird name, this store is quite unusual and definitely worth a gawk. Pretend you are Madonna. You're furnishing your bedroom in the Miami look; you need lots of drippy candles and drapey bend posts—look no further. Peel me a grape.

SOUTH BEACH STYLE
1020 Lincoln Road Mall, Miami Beach.

Don't panic at the name, this store isn't really weird or wired. They claim to sell furniture for the way you live, but mostly it's candles, leopard- or zebra-printed place mats, some furniture, and tabletop design.

DETAILS
1031 Lincoln Road Mall, Miami Beach.

One of the best stores on Lincoln Road, this is sort of a home design shop that has gifts as well as bed and bath items and a little of everything; it's really sort of a lifestyle store. The look is very resort luxe, red velvet sofas with zebra rugs and mosaic planters. Soaps, candles, aromatherapy, cards, teddy bears, leopard-print lamp shades, rag rugs, and oversize bird cages—you get my drift. We certainly aren't in Kansas anymore.

DISH
939 Lincoln Road Mall, Miami Beach.

There are several shops like this in America—not a lot of them, but the store is fantastic if you've never seen one before and merely fun if you're already onto the style of it. Dish, like LouLou's Lost & Found in Boston and Fishs Eddy in New York, sells reproduction and sometimes genuine catering and

hotel supply dishes, complete with logos of whatever restaurants or cafes they once belonged to. I
thought the best item I saw was a Havana cigar
ashtray, but it cost $40, which was beyond me. Cer-
tainly a fun browse.

Lifestyle

I don't know what else to call this category, because
it serves the whole, so I've listed just a few favorite
shops that sell clothes and home items or a combination of clothes and something else. I've created a
different category for spas, which are a specific element of the local lifestyle and certainly part of the
experience, even for a 1-day visit!

Note that I've already written so much about
News Café (800 Ocean Drive, South Beach) that I
won't include it one more time, but this is a lifestyle
kind of place, too—even their logo merchandise has
come to symbolize South Beach.

ISLAND TRADING
1332 Ocean Dr., South Beach.

If SoBe had a dozen stores of this calibre then you'd
have a really good time in South Beach. As it is, this
is about the best in town—a Jamaican, West African, slightly Asian-Orientele lifestyle place selling
clothes, gifts, and tabletop design. Bright, original,
wearable, unique, special. And, you get a discount
if you are staying at the Cavalier, the hotel next door.
Their slogan is "fashion, fabrics, and furnishings
from parts of the world few of us will ever see."
Chris Blackwell is, of course, the genius behind some
of this.

GOLD KIOSK
Hotel Delano, 1685 Collins Ave., Miami Beach.

Gold Kiosk is a small chain of hotel stores developed for the chicer-than-thou Paramount, Royalton,
Mondrian etc. family. They are unlike any other

hotel gift shops you've ever seen—a snazzy blend of European taste and merchandise, periodicals from all over, wild designs, upscale brands of suntan oil, and posh, inventive little nothings that are cutting-edge must-haves. Go here if only as an excuse to explore the Delano. It's a lifestyle thing; either you get it or you don't.

FLOWERS & FLOWERS
925 Lincoln Road Mall, Miami Beach.

A different aspect of the local lifestyle is related to flowers and scent. This shop offers a floral menu, celebrity-oriented baskets of goodies, and assorted candles, home fragrances, and desserts. A fabulous fuddle of stuff that hits the spot.

GAY EMPORIUM
720 Lincoln Road Mall, Miami Beach.

Free condoms and literature.

Malls

Although Miami, like any sprawling American city, has plenty of malls, and some of them are fun to shop or interesting to look at, the easiest ones for a cruise visitor are Bayside and Bal Harbour.

BAL HARBOUR SHOPS
9700 Collins Ave., Bal Harbour.

For a description of the mall, see page 89.
   Tenants include: Ann Taylor, Caché, Chanel, Celine, Jaeger, Laura Ashley, Mondi, Prada, St. John, Ungaro, Hugo Boss, Banana Republic, Brooks Brothers, Gianni Versace, Lacoste, Ralph Lauren/ Polo, Bally, Diego Della Valle, Joan & David, Tiffany & Co., Coach, Fendi, Gucci, Louis Vuitton, Mark Cross, FAO Schwarz, Oilily, Williams-Sonoma, and, for beauty treatments, Georgette Klinger and Jacques Dessange. And that's not even

a full list, that's just for starters. The department store anchors are Neiman-Marcus and Saks Fifth Avenue.

Hours are Monday, Thursday, and Friday, 10am to 9pm; Tuesday, Wednesday, and Saturday, 10am to 6pm; Sunday, noon to 6pm.

Music

SPEC'S MUSIC
Washington Ave. at 5th St., South Beach.

Part of making the scene is hanging and hearin' at this local store for CDs, et al. Open late at night; stock up for the trip if you didn't bring enough tapes.

Plus Sizes

GILDA GEVIS
Loehmann's Fashion Island, 18785 Biscayne Blvd., North Miami Beach.

I wasn't going to give any listings in this part of town because it is more than a schelp for a day-tripper on a cruise, but if you crave different togs for sizes 16 to 24 that are funky, possibly a little ethnic, fun, and highly imaginative, this is worth the trip. There are work clothes, dress-up (good for the cruise), and, of course, weekend, sports, and leisure clothes.

Postcards

Mass market cards cost 10 for $1 at any of the TT's (tourist traps) along the Lincoln Road Mall. My favorite postcards—deco-style drawings of the famous South Beach hotels of the past (some now gone and forgotten)—are sold at **News Café.** They're $1 each, but actually worth it. The designs are by an artist named Woody Vondracek for **Living Dreams, Inc.,** call ☎ 305/532-4131 if you can't find these cards anywhere else.

Spas

AQUA
Delano Hotel, 1635 Collins Ave., Miami Beach.
☎ *800/949-7414.*

The spa portion of the hotel is privately owned—
Madonna is said to be one of the owners. Concep-
tually, the spa was created for women as a private
escape, although you have to check hours carefully
because there are actually times for different sexes
to use the facilities.

    The spa is not huge but is wonderfully intimate
in a special Caribbean/Miami chic way. Everything
inside is hard, clean, and bright white; outside, the
stucco is painted a Mediterranean/Caribbean blue.
You could just stare at the stucco and the sea forever and find heaven in between.

    Yes, they will take day-trippers and nonresidents
of the hotel. Their products are also sold in a small
shop as you enter.

RUSSIAN & TURKISH BATHS
Castle Hotel, 5445 Collins Ave. ☎ *305/867-8313.*

I've never done this, but it was too good to pass
on—a real old-fashioned Russian baths type of place;
call ahead because some times are set aside for men
only. (Oy!)

FOUNTAINEBLEAU
Foutainebleau Resort & Spa, 4441 Collins Ave.,
Miami Beach ☎ *305/538-2000.*

When I was a child, one was blinded by the dazzle
of the Fountainbleau; now it's owned by Hilton and
isn't what it used to be. BUT, it still makes me giggle
and I love it and it's very much the Miami Beach
thing. Yes, it has its own beachside spa, so you can
go for a day or half day and soak up all the glamour
and silliness and enjoy. The hotel is huge, and there
is a shopping mall in the basement when you're done

at the spa. Oh yeah, they even have an in-line skating clinic so you can spend a day here and then skate all night on South Beach, like everyone else.

FT. LAUDERDALE

· ·

Only an hour north of Miami, Fort Lauderdale is a different kind of place. It's also much more suburban and spread out (Miami has spread, but there's an urgency to it). Ft. Lauderdale lacks the energy of downtown Miami or even Miami Beach; South Beach might just as well be on another planet.

It takes some effort to find something to do that's more than merely killing time. Since **The Galleria,** the leading upscale mall in the area, often sends a free shuttle bus to meet incoming ships, most passengers simply take the easy route and head to the mall, which has **Neiman-Marcus, Saks,** and just about every other fancy retailer and chain store you can think of.

Otherwise, you might taxi to one of these destinations and just stroll. Certainly, if you come in for a few days, you'll rent a car and be within easy access of all the suburban shopping parts of Ft. Lauderdale: **Sawgrass Mills,** one of the country's top factory outlet malls; Miami; and even Boca Raton and Palm Beach.

Port Everglades, the Port of Ft. Lauderdale, is off on its own and, however pleasant, is not walking distance to much of anything.

SAWGRASS MILLS
12801 West Sunrise Blvd., Sunrise.

This is a little inland from Ft. Lauderdale in a suburb known as either Sunrise or Plantation; the two are so close to each other that few locals know where each one starts or ends. This outlet mall is a destination unto itself, made even juicer within the last year by the addition of some more upscale shops. Not every single store is an outlet, some are merely "value oriented," but there's everything you can imagine here, from the usual **Polo/Ralph Lauren Factory Store** to **Neiman's Last Call.** That's almost 300 stores! Hours are Monday to Saturday, 10am to 9:30pm; Sunday, 11am to 8pm.

LAS OLAS
Las Olas Blvd.

Las Olas Boulevard is the main shopping street of what was once downtown Ft. Lauderdale, at a time when there was such an old-fashioned notion of a downtown street. The street is still a pleasant stroll. Many of the stores along it sell French Provençale country looks, international crafts, local gallery arts and seascapes, and aromatherapy and bath goods (check out **Goodebodies,** 920 E. Las Olas Blvd., for soaps, bath gels, and massage potions). Cafes and such are on hand for ladies who lunch (I vote for **Mangos,** 904 E. Las Olas Blvd., for something light and simple and fitting the tropical nature of your visit).

Very classy area, and not too touristy. A Las Olas trolley circles downtown.

VOGUE ITALIA
831 E. Las Olas Blvd. (for women),
1018 E. Las Olas Blvd. (for men).

I met a man named Joel on the *Sea Goddess* who told me about this source—it's a discounter for big-name Italian designer clothing. They actually guarantee the lowest prices. If you're looking for anything from **Armani** to **Versace,** you may want to hightail it over here. Open 7 days a week, 11am to 11pm.

A Few Quick Tips

In a survey on love on board ships printed in *Porthole Magazine,* most of the couples surveyed admitted packing sex toys and massage oils for their cruise. If you forgot to do so, check out **Goodebodies.** Erotic chocolates (I don't need to get graphic here, do I?) are available at **Anything in Chocolate,** 1221 East Las Olas Blvd.

And if you have forgotten formal attire for shipboard, try **Maus & Hoffman,** 800 E. Las Olas Blvd.

CAPE CANAVERAL

If you grew up watching "I Dream of Jeannie," then you're familiar with Cocoa Beach and Cape Canaveral. It hasn't changed enormously except for one big thing—**Disney** has moved in and opened up shop. Make that, ship.

Cape Canaveral is about an hour from Orlando, and now that Disney is also in the cruise business, they bus their passengers from the Magic Kingdom and back so that transport is seamless. Everything is organized so perfectly (in the Disney style) that you don't even have time to go shopping. You probably won't even want to go shopping because you're so excited just to be connecting from one park to the next—and yes, the ship is a type of theme park. Don't worry, there will be plenty of stores on board!

Chapter Seven

· · · · · · · · ·

THE BAHAMAS

ANNOUNCEMENT

· ·

You probably know this already—and if you don't, I hate to be the one to break it to you—but the Bahamas are not really in the Caribbean. They're in the Atlantic!

And, getting technical on you, Bermuda is also in the Atlantic. In fact, Bermuda is so far into the Atlantic that it's almost in the Carolinas, so it's not in this book.

But don't panic; I'm not that big on technicalities. If you're headed to the Bahamas, I can talk about it—my editor said so. Scads of cruise passengers go to the Bahamas; in fact, it is the leading destination for cruise ships, and often your only chance to be on foreign soil during your cruise time. So, all ashore that's goin' ashore, we've got shopping to do and a lot of stuff to see and do. No time to swim with the dolphins or wonder why Merv Griffin moved out. I'll be at Atlantis while you read this, so 'cmon down.

WELCOME TO THE BAHAMAS

· ·

Okay, remember these things: beaches, resorts, James Bond, Tony Roma, and shopping, shopping, shopping. The Bahamas considers itself a major shopping destination . . . and many cruise passengers do, too. The islands reclassified their duty-free status in 1992, and the rest is history, well, shopping history anyway.

If you haven't been to the Bahamas in a few years, you'll find that prices are significantly less than they used to be, with the decreases differing in various categories of goods. Among those categories where goods have been reduced because of the change in duty laws are liquor, perfume, and jewelry. Cigarettes are still taxed.

For the most part, I haven't really noticed that price is the real issue, or that anybody cares about what changes have been made. For many, this is simply the first stop on a cruise, or the first serious shopping port (possibly the *only* serious shopping port). I've seen people swarm off the ship like worker bees and pour themselves into downtown Nassau.

Nassau, by the way, is on New Providence Island and is merely one of several hundred Bahamian islands in the confederation. Paradise Island is just a sneeze away and is discussed in the "Neighborhoods" section of this chapter.

There is more to New Providence Island than just downtown Nassau. While the major "General Stores" and the big perfume shops and the hustle and the bustle are in this downtown area, other parts of town aren't so congested and may be a little dressier, or less touristy, depending on your needs. Nothing is far away and you should have ample time to get to a few shopping destinations before you wreck your credit rating.

NASSAU NEIGHBORHOODS

Your ship arrives at Prince George Wharf right in the heart of downtown Nassau.

Downtown

Downtown Nassau is the main shopping area, and Bay Street is the main drag. I won't tell you it's quaint or cute or fancy or charming. I will tell you that I love the horse-drawn carriages and that there is a certain air of energy that many other Caribbean destinations don't have.

The most intense shopping area is clustered around the British Colonial Hotel and works its way to Rawson Square. Shops do continue along Bay Street, the main drag, past the Moses Shopping Mall, but the big-interest browse stops there.

I have walked from downtown to Paradise Island and found it a pleasant 2½-mile jaunt, but the only secret vendors you'll pass along the way are the fresh fruits and fish marketeers and conch shell sellers at the base of the bridge at Potter's Cay. If it's hot, this might not be the best way to spend the day. Most people seem to be happy staying downtown, but it's not the only game in town.

Paradise Island

If downtown isn't swanky, Paradise Island is. Attached to town by a toll bridge (you pay even if you walk over it), Paradise Island has its own casino, clubs, and hotels, and even a Club Med. All the hotels have shopping arcades; a wonderful little Paradise Village Shopping Center of some 20-odd stores is all very clean and pretty and pleasant. Some of the stores are branches of downtown stores; some are not.

A pale-peach stucco series of bungalows in the California-Caribbean style of architecture, the Paradise Village Shopping Center is just over the bridge and dead ahead when you hit Paradise Island. You can walk there from many of the nearby hotels.

The center appears to be small, but has several hidden buildings and many backdoor stores—don't give up until you've seen it all. There are even some big-name designer shops here. It's all very neat, clean, cheery, and perfect for tourists as well as locals. Stock up on suntan oil, newspapers, books, dried apricots, T-shirts, and Louis Feraud.

Paradise Wines & Spirits sells a tremendous amount of beer, but also has liquor and bottled water; the **Perfume Bar** is large, with an excellent stock of fragrances; **Three Sisters** has Hong Kong bargains on Hong Kong– and China-made linens.

Pipe of Peace opens at 8:30am so you can get in some shopping before you go off on another adventure—buy beach fashions, running shorts, bathing suits, and fashions you can actually use when you get back home. **Francesca's** sells Louis Feraud as well as Hanes and Vanity Fair—this is a very elegant boutique that isn't at all vacation-oriented or hokey. Some of the stores are open on Sunday.

Cable Beach

The advantage to Cable Beach is that it is so close to the airport, yet still on the beach, away from the dullness of downtown's antiglitter and yet not far from town, should you care to go shopping. (Of course you care!) While Cable Beach shopping is not as sophisticated as on Paradise Island, there are individual hotel stores as well as a 22-store arcade at the Cable Beach Hotel. Don't miss a look at the first hotel and casino on the beach (built by the cruise line Carnival), the Crystal Palace, now named **The Nassau Marriott Resort & Crystal Palace Casino.** Of course it's filled with shops, it's a virtual mall of interconnecting buildings designed by one of the most famous cruise-ship designers of modern times, Joe Farcas.

HEY, MON

Nassau has some of the best T-shirt energy in the Caribbean. As a result you'll see great designs, lots of choices, good prices, and much competition and have a ball buying Ts. Don't pay more than $10; $8 is more like it, for a good shirt. Most expensive

Ts are the ones with puff designs; look for multi-T deals, like three shirts for $10, in nonpuff designs that might not be the last word in style. The **Straw Market** has the best buys, but check quality carefully. The more you buy, the more you bargain.

GETTING AROUND

If you come by plane, taxis meet you at the airport and have set prices. Try bargaining or teaming up with a fellow traveler or two. Otherwise, you will be met by a car or van from your resort only if you have arranged for this service before arrival. Some people on package deals come clutching taxi vouchers—they get a free ride to their vacation home.

If you come via cruise ship, you dock just about downtown and can do the downtown shopping area on foot.

There are cute little vans (jitneys) that serve as buses for locals; you can get one in town in Nassau. They usually cost 75¢ to $1, depending on how far you are going. If you have nothing else to do and want an inexpensive tour of the island, this is a great way to do it.

There are also horse-drawn carriages that can give you a tour or a ride; the horses wear these adorable straw hats and offer many photo ops. I almost expect to see them in Mickey Mouse ears next time I'm in town, as a tribute to the Disney fleet.

If you're looking for a taxi to get you away from the heart of town and into some of the other areas, find one near St. George's Wharf or at the British Colonial Hotel.

Also note that if you just want to get out, about, and see something different, there's a ferry at Rawson Square that will take you to Paradise Island for $2. Buy a round-trip ticket if you are planning on returning to the ship (though you may want to jump ship and stay forever); round-trip is $3.

ABOUT ADDRESSES

Few stores have actual addresses, or if they do, the buildings are not well marked. Never mind, mon. Most downtown addresses are on Bay Street or one of the downtown cross streets within a block of where that street intersects with Bay. Seek and ye shall find . . . and buy.

STORE HOURS

Stores are open Monday to Friday, 9am to 5pm and on Saturday, 8:30am to 5:30pm. Some stores close at noon on Thursdays. Go figure.

Many stores on Bay Street are open Sundays. On Sundays, also check out hotel gift shops and the Straw Markets.

MONEY MATTERS

Official currency is the Bahamian dollar which is on par with the U.S. dollar. Try to use U.S. money or credit cards whenever possible.

BEST BUYS

Booze   Up with rum, by gum.

British Goods   Tons of 'em, from English antiques to jumpers (sweaters) to St. Michael's brand, aside from Bermuda this is one of the most "veddy, veddy" islands. More "veddy" than Barbados.

China & Crystal   Same prices as St. Thomas without the same duty-free advantages.

Jewelry   All this jewelry, especially gold and then emeralds, makes me nervous because there's so much of it and everyone is going hog-wild for it.

Watches   Best bet ever.

WATCH OUT

Be careful with perfume and cosmetics prices—not only price-wise but quality-wise. Remember that these goods can easily be faked, so buy from reputable stores. If you care if the fragrance is made with denatured alcohol or not, ask. If you want a potato alcohol fragrance, make sure it has been imported from France, not Miami.

Also avoid buying cameras, electronics goods, and toys that are best bought at reputable discounters in the U.S. **John Bull** is a reputable store and the best on the island for cameras; they have expert salespeople and will help you, but don't pounce unless you know exactly what you are doing, and what prices are at home.

LANDLUBBER'S DELIGHT

GREYCLIFF
West Hill St., Nassau. ☎ *800/423-4095 in the U.S., or 242/322-2796; fax 242/326-6110.*

Yes, it was the famous American designer Adolfo who first taught me about Greycliff, the fanciest mansion turned tiny hotel in town. Even if you just come for a meal, this is the true lifestyle of the rich and famous. No autographs please.

COMPASS POINT
West Bay St., Nassau. ☎ *800/OUTPOST in the U.S., or 242/327-4500; fax 242/327-3299.*

Chris Blackwell made the moola in music but has gone into the hotel business throughout the Caribbean and Miami Beach area. His Nassau hotel is the stuff of which photo ops are made and is a series of picture perfect little two story A-frame bungalow things that are so adorable you may consider jumping ship and moving in. If you're just in town for a day, come take a look and eat—the restaurant is a well-known local watering hole.

ROYAL BAHAMIAN HOTEL
West Bay St., Nassau. ☎ *800/SANDALS or 242/327-6400; fax 242/327-1894.*

If you prefer old English colonial elegant and a little bit hidden and a little bit of a surprise, then this is the property for you. The location isn't that central but for getting away from tourists and downtown, you can't beat it. Prices are also moderate considering that this is one of those all-inclusive resorts run by Sandals.

ATLANTIS
Casino Dr., Paradise Island. ☎ *800/321-3000 or 242/363-3000; fax 242/363-3957.*

Not to date myself, but I liked it here when Merv Griffin owned it and there were banana leaves printed on the carpet. Things have gotten a lot jazzier since Sun International bought out Merv and brought in the dolphins. The hotel must now be considered one of the wonders of the world; see it even if you aren't staying here—you can come back another day. This is a themed attraction with casino and hotel ammenities and shopping that is the core of Paradise Island, although there are other casinos and hotels around. Expensive, but there are inclusive packages.

DOWNTOWN SHOPPING CENTERS
. . . .

Most of the shopping centers in Nassau are glorified passages, but almost all of them are worth wandering down and around:

Prince George Plaza The first shopping center closest to the wharf and loaded with TTs (tourist traps) and Gucci.

The Nassau Question: Where to Shop, Freeport or Nassau?

Those who cruise to both Freeport and Nassau often wonder which port will offer the best shopping, and don't know where to pounce first. So here it is, the truth: Freeport has parts that are cuter than Nassau, but Nassau has a better shopping selection. Prices are uniform on both islands, except in the markets where you need to bargain anyway. Because Nassau is the better shopping area, it is covered exclusively in these pages.

Moses Shopping Plaza Just as downtown Bay Street seems to be petering out, you'll come to the Moses Shopping Plaza, which is new and modern and leased full of big names like **Stefanel** and **Benetton.** There's also a drugstore for basic needs, a health-food market, and a fabulous fancy underwear store, appropriately named **Posh Lingerie.** The shop selling sewing notions and yarn is probably meant for locals, but if you are knitting on the cruise, you may want to stop in.

British Colonial Forming a ring around one side of the entrance to the British Colonial Hotel, right on Bay Street, is an arcade of stores that includes a few restaurants (and a McDonald's). There's a minimarket, a few boutiques, and a branch of **Mademoiselle,** a women's ready-to-wear shop.

Nassau International Center It's not much of a bazaar, or much of a shopping center, but this little passage of shops is fun to look at and does host a few stores that sell top-of-the-line European fashions. Located at the intersection of Charlotte Street.

Colony Place Another passage, this one new and stucco-y, with 12 shops including a bake shop. There's also a little stand for food, a shoe store, a jewelry shop, a T-shirt shop, and more. Good marks for shopping cutes.

THE LAY OF THE LAND/NASSAU

The center of town is actually Rawson Square, which is bordered by the cruise pier (Prince George Wharf) at one end and government buildings and the library on the other side. Seemingly, Bay Street starts at no. 1, which is the pale pink stucco old-timer, the British Colonial Hotel.

The side streets coming of Bay Street all have shops, and locals claim that Charlotte Street is the Bond Street of Nassau. Hmmm, well maybe the New Bond Street . . . or the James Bond Street. Well, there are some antique shops on the back streets and other shops that might not look like much from the outside, but turn out to be quite deep and filled with wonders.

Real people stores, which dot the way, sell inexpensive ready-to-wear or less-than-designer shoes and are probably not what you came here to see but can be a fun browse.

NASSAU RESOURCES

Antiques & Collectibles

FRANCIS PECK LTD.
George St.

Although the sign over the door says "Antiques," the shop sells mostly porcelain and a lot of **Herend.** Some is old, some is not so old. All of it is fabulous.

The store closes from 1 to 2pm daily (for lunch) and closes for good at noon on Friday. It is not open at all on weekends. Collectors and serious shoppers will adore this treasure.

COIN OF THE REALM
Charlotte St. at Bay St.

Coins and stamps as well as unusual fine jewelry; set off the main street.

MARLBOROUGH ANTIQUES
Queen St. at Marlborough St.

Traditional English antiques; really neat, old local photos.

BALMAIN ANTIQUES
Mason's Blvd. and Charlotte St., Apt. No. 2F.

Ignore the French name, mostly English antiques.

Beachwear

THE NASSAU SHOP
Bay St.

A lot like a department store, the Nassau Shop has a counter that sells English sweaters at London prices, a few counters that sell perfumes and cosmetics, and a mezzanine for linens. The women's department has a small but excellent selection of shorts and tops that are good for back home.

MADEMOISELLE
Bay St.

Mademoiselle sells inexpensive and mostly American-made sportswear that is probably bought in Miami at the Mart. But there are choices here that you don't get in your hometown, and prices run from inexpensive to moderate. While the store is sort of for locals, it's also worth a peek if you want resort clothes at affordable prices. Accessories as well as a selection of batiks are also in evidence.

Now then, as for those body and massage oils— the ones that the "sex at sea survey" says you have

already brought along or will buy on the trip—here
is your store.

British Goods

ST. MICHAEL SHOP
Market St. at Duke St.

This rust-colored stucco shop is the Marks & Spen-
cer outlet in the Caribbean. The St. Michael underwear is always worthwhile; otherwise, this is not a
fashion hot spot. Funky though, and I happen to
like it.

ENGLISH SPORTS & SWEATER SHOP
Bay St. at Charlotte St.

Preppy heaven right here in Nassau, though the
Androsia line of locally made batik fashions gives it
a touch of the Caribe. If you walk into a sale, you'll
pay Hong Kong prices for traditional Shetland
sweaters; Burberry raincoats are also a good buy.
For ready-to-wear that you can wear at home, and
on a cruise, this is one of the best stores around.

THE SCOTTISH SHOP
Charlotte St.

Another of the several local mini-department stores,
this one is stocked to the gills with Scottish things—
fabrics, kilts, and even Edinburgh crystal. It may be
hard to think wool in this kind of climate, but you'll
find this is one of the most complete shops on the
island and offers fair prices. They also mail order.

General Stores

LITTLE SWITZERLAND
Bay St.

One of my favorite stores in Nassau, hell, in the
whole of the Caribbean as well. Little Switzerland,
as everyone knows, is one of those general stores

that sells a little of everything but is fancy and reputable and a pleasure to shop, even though it does get crowded. Perfumes and cosmetics; departments for china and crystal are more to the rear; there's an excellent selection of Lladro and Belleek and all the big names. Branch stores in most of the hotels and in other parts of town.

JOHN BULL
Bay St.

One of the better general stores of Nassau, John Bull is not teeming with china and Lladro statues but does a quiet and impressive business in designer (Rolex, Piaget, Heuer, Ebel) watches, pens, cameras, and more. Those fabulous Porsche sunglasses are sold here for a little less than in the United States. There are five stores on the island, but the best is the Bay Street flagship.

TREASURE TRADERS
Bay St.

You can trade in the vacation and just pitch the tent right here if you like fancy stores that look like the right place to buy wedding presents. The store doesn't have the same young energy that Solomon's Mines has, although they sell a lot of the same merchandise, including every big name in china, crystal, and gifts from all over the world, not just England and France. Some crystal pieces from Scandinavia are outstanding bargains.

Jewelry

All of the general stores sell tons of jewelry and are often the official distributors for the biggest brands of watches and jewelry.

DISCOUNT GOLD MINE
Bay St. at East St.

You cannot miss this shop, especially if you have kids or teens with you. We're not sure if it's a Disneyland type of creation or genuine, but the store appears to be built into a mine shaft complete with dripping water, rock walls, the works. It's a must-see. The merchandise is very average Hong Kong and Italian fare—chains, charms, standard styles in earrings. Prices are excellent.

GOLD
Bay St. at Straw Market.

They weigh the jewelry to determine the price. You get a little card with the item weight, the price per gram, the total price, and the date all printed in. Gold guarantees the lowest prices on the island, and you have 48 hours to make an exchange or get your money back if you find a better deal. We've found a lot of high-fashion styles here and always come back—almost directly from the cruise ship—to soak up the New York wheeling and dealing and good-value vibrations. There are many, many jewelry shops on Bay Street, but this one is a favorite.

Leather Goods

BRASS & LEATHER SHOP
Charlotte St.

A small, dark boutique selling big-name Italian leather goods, but too expensive for me. Do serious homework and know you're saving on one particular style.

FENDI
Charlotte St. at Bay St.

I think it's real but I don't think I can afford it.

GUCCI
Saffrey Sq. on Bay St. at Bank Lane.

I have bought items at this Gucci and been pleased with them, but I think this is Caribbean Gucci and not Italian Gucci, if you get my drift.

Perfumes

LIGHTBOURN'S
Bay St. at George St.

The perfect island retreat, complete with a pineapple on the old-fashioned signpost. (A pineapple is the sign of welcome.) Lightbourn's has so many perfumes and cosmetics that your nose will start to burn after you're here for a half hour. Prices on goods are uniform throughout the island, but the selection here is good.

THE BEAUTY SPOT
Bay St.

Fabulous perfume shop with adjoining cosmetic boutique for Lancôme, Arden, and Lauder lines. Great fun, great help, and expert makeup advice. Prices are posted; they specialize in gift bottles of famous names priced at $25 and less. Prices on these items are the same all over the island, so if you're choosing for the fun of it—this one is fun. It may be crowded.

CAMEO
West Bay St. at Straw Market.

This store carries La Prairie, one of the few sources in the Caribbean for this Swiss treatment line. Also has other European brands of makeup and beauty cures in stock.

Personal Needs

You'll find just about everything you need on Bay Street, but sometimes you don't want to search too much. If it's film selection you seek, the largest selection is carried at John Bull, one of the general stores toward the far end of Bay Street (see above).

DOCKSIDE WAREHOUSE
Rawson Sq.

Everything you want in the first store you see when you set foot on shore—suntan oil, T-shirts, towels, shorts, and more. Excellent prices geared for tourists and cruisers; many promotional items.

CITY PHARMACY LTD.
Bay St.

Watch out for the price of Revlon nail polish (higher than in the U.S. when we were there), but stop here for a little of everything else, from toiletries to toys. There's a real pharmacy in the back, a candy selection for your kids, some British toy soldiers, and a fair selection of fragrances. Toys are upstairs. This is the kind of place nonshoppers like for emergency buying.

Porcelain & Dishes

The general stores all carry china, crystal, porcelain, dishes, and all sorts of goods, English and otherwise.

THE PORCELAIN GALLERY
Maritime House, Frederick St.

Very nice, very swank store that doesn't sell the big names in porcelain, but does sell different brands that you may have never heard of, like Kaiser porcelain. It's worth a peek. There's an antique store next door.

Straw Markets

First, a few general rules:

- Look at everything before you pounce.
- Bargain for the best prices. Don't be surprised if someone says to you, "How much do you want to pay?"
- Check the quality on the T-shirts; some of them may be off-register.
- Don't pay the asking price for anything.
- Pay attention to the stitches and styles of the workmanship; some of the women invent their own stitches, and much of the workmanship is downright unbelievable.
- Don't miss the back scratcher made of plastic in the shape of a British bobby.
- Straw should be very flexible and very strong. It's durable and should be able to roll in a ball without being babied. Ask if you can test items. Straw makes a good tote because it can hold a lot of weight without giving way.
- If you think you're going to see markets like this all over the Caribbean and are tempted to wait for another one, forget it, unless you go to a smaller and more authentic market outside of town. There is no other property like this in all the other islands.

THE STRAW MARKET
Downtown Nassau.

Perhaps the most highly touted of tourist shopping sites in the islands, the downtown Straw Market is not the only one in town, it's just the most well known and the one where "everyone" goes.

Although Nassau stores close up tight on Sunday, fret no more—the Straw Market is open 7 days a week, and you really don't need anyplace else to shop in town.

Maybe they don't sell china and crystal and perfume, but the booth-after-booth carnival atmosphere just does something to our blood. There are two tiers to the Straw Market; upstairs more local crafts are sold than straw. Downstairs is mostly T-shirts and straw goods.

I bought one of those giant tote bags and asked the maker to embroider "BORN TO SHOP: CARIBBEAN" and paid an extra $2 for all the stitching. If you just want your name or the words "BORN TO SHOP" on a bag, it should be free. Prices are very competitive because so much of the merchandise is similar.

STRAW MARKET
Cable Beach.

Much smaller and funkier version of the above.

Chapter Eight

· · · · · · ·

THE AMERICAN CARIBBEAN: PUERTO RICO

WELCOME TO SAN JUAN

· ·

Okay, cut it out right now—no refrains from *West Side Story,* no wisecracks or cha cha cha jokes. Not only is San Juan a certain kind of fabulous, but the city is bidding for the 2004 Olympics, which, if successful, would make it the first Latin America host since Mexico City in 1968. The competition is stiff, but the facts are real: San Juan has arrived.

San Juan has a great airport that serves as the hub for the Caribbean; it's got a marvelous pier facility—still being improved—and perhaps the best tourist Old Town in the Basin. Other islands have old towns, but they are funky (sometimes *too* funky) and Old San Juan has been redone with pride and prejudice—prejudice toward shoppers!

So look out, guys: Whether your cruise starts in San Juan or whether you're there for a day or a week, you'll find some pleasant surprises. Stick with me.

And now, surprise number one: San Juan, make that Puerto Rico, is a Commonwealth of the United States of America. Read on for what that means to you as a shopper. Surprise number two: There are tons of factory outlets in San Juan, with more coming on board. If you're dreaming of handicrafts and straw hats and colors like turquoise and coral, well, yes, San Juan has those things; but did you know that San Juan has one of the best **Ralph Lauren/Polo Factory Store** branches you are ever going to see?

A COMMONWEALTH OF IDEAS

Puerto Rico is a commonwealth and considered part of the United States of America. It's not quite a state but has many of the same rights, and it, too, has a governor. If you're going to Puerto Rico from the continental United States, you have no customs formalities, and you are not entering a duty-free zone or free port.

If you are returning to the U.S. through San Juan—this is common with many cruise ships—you will go through customs and immigration in San Juan because this is your official point of entry into the U.S.

There is no $400 duty-free allowance when you return from Puerto Rico. There is no limit on the amount of booze you can buy. There's no nuttin', and don't let any fast talkin' con artist try to convince you of anything else.

There is a duty-free store at the pier for those who will leave by ship, and this is a real duty free; any other duty free on land is merely a con.

THE PONCE DE LEÓN RULE OF SHOPPING

Because there are basically no bargains in San Juan (except for in the outlet stores), and because a large portion of Old San Juan's business comes from tourists who are passing through on cruise ships, the vendors of Old San Juan have gotten together to offer you incentives to buy from them. It's not unusual for a salesperson to say to you, "Our prices are the same as in St. Thomas," or for a vendor to say, "I'll take off 10%; that will make this the same price in St. Thomas. You can't get it any cheaper."

Why wait for St. Thomas? Indeed, it may not pay for you to wait. Consider these facts and buy in San Juan when:

- You're in American factory outlets that will ship at UPS rates.
- You can't live without the item another moment.
- You're saving your duty-free allowance for another purchase because you can buy as much as you want in Puerto Rico and not worry about duty allowances. (Shopper's note: If you are leaving the United States from Puerto Rico and have bought heavily in Puerto Rico, save receipts to prove to U.S. Customs officials that you bought those items within the U.S.)

LOCAL PRICES

Prices in San Juan are expensive, for good reason: San Juan is the business center of the Caribbean. San Juan deals in a lot of American-made merchandise that has to be shipped in—even though Miami isn't far, you pay for transportation. And many goods come from farther away than Miami.

San Juan is the big time; it's a real city: It looks and feels like a city and offers city services. Business is booming. There are no bargains unless you know where to look for them. On the whole, figure that prices in San Juan are 10% higher than elsewhere in the Basin.

MONEY MATTERS

As part of the U.S., Puerto Rico trades in the U.S. dollar. Most stores, even the grocery store Pueblo, take credit cards.

BEST BUYS OF SAN JUAN

. . . .

The thing to stock up on in San Juan, which you might need for a trip around the Caribbean, is books from American publishing companies. These can cost a fortune in a Caribbean resort, but you'll pay only their marked retail price in Puerto Rico. The bad news: periodicals are expensive—a 50¢ newspaper can cost $2; it has to be flown in, so you pay!

There are several excellent bookstores in San Juan—so stock up. Try: **Bell, Book & Candle,** 102 De Diego, Santurce; **Parentesis** at Plaza Las Americas; **B. Dalton** at Plaza Carolina; **The Book Store,** 255 San Jose, Old San Juan (which is the largest bookshop in town and is certainly along your path). Drugstores and grocery stores also carry paperbacks.

Another bargain is postcards and stamps. If you send your postcards from outside the U.S., you will pay approximately 40¢ to 50¢ each in postage and must send them airmail and pray that they get delivered. If you send them from Puerto Rico (or the U.S. Virgin Islands), you use a regular 20¢ stamp and you know the U.S. Post Office can be trusted to deliver the goods. Also note that stores, such as the **Ralph Lauren / Polo Factory Store,** can mail your purchases to you and you can trust the mail!

Jewelry can be a good buy in San Juan, especially if you can bargain in a fancy jewelry store by explaining that you're on a cruise and are expecting a serious bargain—ask to match prices offered on other islands.

If you discover that you have left home some vital element of your cruise wardrobe, San Juan may be the place to fill in the missing pieces. Prices for basics, such as ready-to-wear and bathing suits, are very high on cruise ships and in most resort areas of the islands. Stop by one of the outlet stores, discounters, or off-pricers in San Juan to get that suit or pair of stockings or undies you left back home.

GETTING AROUND

. . . .

If you come in by cruise ship, you can walk everywhere you need to go in Old San Juan. You needn't worry about the rest of the city, unless you want to go to the beach. Many cruise ships offer add-on San Juan packages of 2 or 3 days at a resort at excellent prices.

If your ship is based in San Juan and this is your point of embarkation and disembarkation, ships will also provide transportation from the San Juan airport to the ship. However, if the bus to the airport is at a set time and until then you'll just be sitting around, it pays to have a half day booked at a local hotel or to even get a little independent on your own. The cruise pier is so incredibly convenient to everything you want to see and do in Old San Juan that you should arrange your travels to take advantage of this.

If you go independent for a few hours or for your transfer to the airport, you will probably need to take a few taxis. *Warning:* Do not get in a taxi whose meter is not working. Ask if there is a fixed fare. Take down the driver's name and number from his posted license if you have any trouble. If you're taking a taxi from the cruise pier—where the cabs are all in a long line waiting for you—do not set foot in the cab without insisting on the meter. Don't fall for the old "My meter is broken" routine.

THE LAY OF THE LAND

. . . .

Since the cruise piers and Old San Juan's touristic, cultural, and shopping delights are all in the same area, you need not really even understand the geography of San Juan or this part of Puerto Rico. Use the map on page 41 to get your bearings; Old San Juan operates on a grid system and you will have no trouble prowling around. If it's too hot to cope, there are shuttle buses.

Most of the ships dock in the main Port Authority area of Old San Juan, which is a fabulous location for tourists and shoppers. However, every now and then, but not very often, ships leave from Pier 17, which is not in the same area of town. To get to Old San Juan from Pier 17, simply take any public bus (25¢, exact change) to the last stop, which is a mini-terminal across the street from the main pier. While you could walk this distance (it's a little more than one mile), the neighborhood between Pier 17 and Old San Juan is not considered safe.

There are two main terminals, almost next door to each other, which get the majority of the big ships. Each has an office for making international phone calls, as well as a large and well-stocked tourist shop that sells many little gifty items and an additional duty-free store that sells mostly booze but has some perfumes and other luxury goods. Wait on the perfume, but buy booze now if you want it for your ship's cabin. Remember, drinks on board are usually about $5 each, and $10 will buy you a full bottle of just about anything at the duty free.

Next to the terminal is the Tourist Office, where they will give you a free map of Old San Juan. They do not have much information on shopping, but you'll have no trouble learning the ropes or getting around.

SAN JUAN NEIGHBORHOODS

. . . .

Old San Juan

Of all the Caribbean cities you will visit, none has the power of Old San Juan because none is as organized, as revitalized, and as professionally done. It's not Disneyland, but hidden in the back streets there are moments to be had, and felt.

In fact, nothing can take away from me a sensory memory of a recent visit when my taxi came into Old San Juan from the side, along the sea, and skirted around for the rear approach to Calle del

Cristo rather than cut into the heart of town and tourists and traffic.

This approach made me realize the true power of the area—the sea, the old houses, the beautiful colors, the restorations, the flowers, the beauty of it all . . . the perfection of a small piece of restored and honed charm. Okay, so I fell for it. So sue me.

Like most old cities, Old San Juan is right on the water, on a little isthmus of land stretching out from the area that has become Condado. The city was, in its past, surrounded by a protective wall and protected by several forts. Parts of all of these remain. The Atlantic Ocean is on one side of Old San Juan; the Caribbean Sea is on the bay side. (The port with the ships is actually on the San Juan Bay side.)

Whether you are in town for the day, to meet up with your cruise ship, or for a major vacation, all stores lead home, and all visitors owe it to themselves to prowl these ancient streets with credit cards in hand.

It's Old San Juan that has the shopping, the colonial buildings in the whitewashed stucco, the red-tiled roofs, the free piña coladas with every $10 purchase. It's Old San Juan that now even has **Marshall's!**

Condado

The Condado area surrounds the Condado Lagoon and includes the lagoon and its wide, gorgeous bridge. I just love it when my taxi soars across the bridge and I see the lagoon, the ocean, and the Hilton Caribe in one quick, loving glance. I have been having a love affair with the Hilton Caribe (say *Caree-bay*) for dozens of years and to me, part of the joy of San Juan is this little jaunt.

Condado is adjacent to Old San Juan and is within walking distance. And that's why the Hilton people built the most famous hotel in the Caribbean right where it is. You can actually walk to all the shopping spots in San Juan (except the mall) from the Hilton, but I never do; it's often too hot, and I'm always too impatient.

Condado is a swank neighborhood filled with posh hotels, many of which have shopping arcades. The Hilton's arcade has about 20 shops and is considered a shopping thrill stop for locals as well as visitors. Ashford Avenue, the main high-ticket shopping drag for locals, is in the Condado neighborhood; the Convention Center is also in this area. Welcome *Yanquis*.

Hato Rey

Most tourist will not even need to know about Hato Rey. **Plaza Las Americas** is the name of the jumbo American-style mall in San Juan's Hato Rey district that serves the same social purposes as every city's best mall. It also acts as the flagship for many stores that have other branches—but are looking their best in the mall. If you are just in town for a few hours via cruise ship, stick to Old San Juan; but if you are in need of a serious shopping fix, come here.

The street that leads to the mall, Avenue Franklin Delano Roosevelt, is dotted with shops (for TV, electronics, shoe repair) and a few outlets and strip centers. This is uptown shopping for locals, but unless you have errands to do, you probably won't need to stop at the rest of the area stores. But you never know.

The mall itself has a **Pueblo** grocery store at one end and all the regular stores you'd expect within.

Cerromar

Cerromar is the out-of-the-way swank part of town where resorts for people who don't want to be close to shopping or cruise ships or tourists are located. The kids love the water playground; you can shop the hotel arcades or stop by Carolina, a suburb of San Juan that's closer to the airport. Carolina has its own shopping mall, **Plaza Carolina,** but the mall isn't as good as Las Americas. But it's not bad either—modern and clean.

Cataño

Location of the Bacardi Rum Factory, across the bay from Old San Juan, see page 140.

LANDLUBBER'S DELIGHT

· ·

Travel to and from a cruise ship can be so stressful that I invariably book a few days at the point of departure or arrival, so that I can really chill out and shop without extra pressure.

HILTON CARIBE & CASINO
Calle Los Rosales (near Ft. San Jéronimo),
San Juan. ☎ *800/HILTONS, or* ☎ *800/468-8585,*
or ☎ *787/721-0303.*

I always add on at least 1 day to my San Juan travels because I adore sitting in the sand at the Hilton Caribe and consider it the perfect piece of perfection to top off a cruise.

While this is not the fanciest hotel in town, it's got a feel that I find very comfortable—from the open-air bar to the tiny private beach to the shopping mall of gift shops. Don't laugh, but I have a spiritual connection to this place and its view of the old fortress, its sea walls, its surf, and the color of the sea.

Almost all rooms have a view; there is a casino if you can't stop gambling. There is a special program for women traveling alone so that you can have a room on a designated floor that guarantees additional security.

On top of all this, the hotel is not very expensive. Often your cruise ship will offer a promotional rate or a package price. I booked it straight through the Hilton main reservation number and was pleased with my summer special rate of $149. In season, rates are $250 to $350, but even then, there are promotions and deals. This hotel was made to win your heart and to do so at a pleasant price; it has an attitude toward price structure many other Hilton hotels do not have and therein lies much of its charm.

I also eat on property because the location is not within the heart of town. In fact, I usually have room service so I can watch the sunset from my room (pure heaven). If I'm with others, I walk to the edge of the property where there's a little seafood hut restaurant on the water, and we eat lobster and talk about how lucky we are.

Ritz Carlton San Juan Hotel & Casino
6961 State Rd. 187. ☎ *800/241-3333.*

This hotel, slated to open in fall 1997, does not have as good a location as the Hilton and it is a lot more expensive, but if you have to have luxury or die, well, go ahead.

Ritz-Carlton is moving into the Caribbean to come on strong and fill a need that they think still exists. This new hotel is 10 stories high and includes a spa just made for indulgence; there's the usual casino as well—a first for the Ritz-Carlton people. There's beach (of course) and many leisure activities. Ask about transportation into town or to Old San Juan, but you'll probably never want to leave the property to face the real world.

LATE DEPARTURES

If you have not booked a hotel room, even for a half-day program, check to see what your cruise line has arranged for you. Some expect you to sit at the airport until your flight, which could be hours away;

others expect you to fend for yourself if you want to amuse yourself before a late departure. Some offer shore excursions that will take you on a tour and then drop you directly at the airport. Royal Carribean Cruise Line has a Crown & Anchor Club at 257 Calle San Justo, walking distance from the piers. The club provides a hospitality suite and place to hang.

PERSONALLY YOURS

For real people needs, there's a pharmacy, drugstore, and grocery store right off the square in Old San Juan; pick from **Puerto Rico Drug, Pueblo** market, or **Walgreen's,** all conveniently located at Plaza Las Armas. There's also a Marshall's here as well.

All ships do sell some sundries on board, but prices on shore will be better.

Also note that if you drink bottled water (a good idea on a cruise ship) or even lots of soft drinks, you may want to load up in San Juan before departure. Soft drinks and small bottles of water on board are often $2.50 each!

SNACK & SHOP

EL CONVENTO HOTEL
100 Calle del Cristo.

Great location on Calle del Cristo in the heart of the shopping; great ambience, since this hotel was once indeed a convent; and great, simple meals such as burgers and the like, enjoyed on the patio, *señora.* It has been closed for renovations (*sí,* to the tune of $15 million yankee smackeroos) and is newly reopened for the 1997 season. Fabulous for a sleep-over, for a honeymoon, and for a taste of Old San Juan.

OLD SAN JUAN RESOURCES
· ·

Art Galleries

There are quite a few galleries in Old San Juan; try:

COLBIRO GRAPHICS
156 Calle del Cristo

GALERIA BOTELLO
208 Calle del Cristo

GALERIA GOTAY
212 Calle San Francisco

GALERIA LABIOSA
200 Calle del Cristo

Artisans

While you won't find the raw folk arts that you get in Mexico, Latin America, and even other islands, you'll find some individual specialists who do some incredibly interesting work.

THE BUTTERFLY PEOPLE
152 Calle La Fortaleza.

Lucite-frame arrangements of real butterflies in the most amazing wall hangings. The store in South Street Seaport in New York City has been a success, and now they've come to Old San Juan. You have to go up some stairs, but it's worth it; prices begin at $20, but the fabulous stuff can cost thousands. Yes, the butterflies are all real, but they're not free.

M. RIVIERA
107 Calle del Cristo.

This shop has about the best $1 gift you'll find any-where in the world: a matchbox created like one of the old houses in Old San Juan. The artist himself is on hand to paint little stucco miniatures of the houses. Quite charming.

PUERTO RICO ARTS & CRAFTS
204 Calle La Fortaleza.

This is almost a jungle of arts and crafts with a cafe in the rear and some good fun to be had in the browsing.

Beachwear

WET
150 Calle Cruz.

In an old house on the real people side of Old San Juan, a little bit away from the main tourist areas (yeah!) and with an unerring eye toward resort chic, be it the brightly colored Jams line to the linen neutrals of the Flax label. Check out the line called Island to Island, which comes from St. Kitts. Chic, practical, and not too expensive.

PUSSER'S COMPANY STORE
202 Calle del Cristo.

By some quirk of shopping real estate, most of the best stores in town are within a block or two of each other on Calle del Cristo. So it is that Pusser's, named for a gin company, is across the street from Ralph Lauren and offers that take-your-breath-away combination of wearable sports, sun, and beachwear; great display of the merchandise; quality goods; and fun stuff for gifts. I fell in love with the enamel tinwares, mugs, cups, plates, etc. with pictures of sailing ships on them and old gin bottle logos. Great gift for $10. There is an outlet store in St. Thomas, but don't wait. Oh yes, check out the lime aftershave—it's unisex enough for men and women, has a stunning bright green bottle and makes a terrific gift as well.

Books

See Best Buys of San Juan, page 126.

Booze

See Rum, page 139.

Cult Heroes

SEÑOR FROGS
203 Calle La Fortaleza; 265 Calle San Francisco;
109 Calle La Fortaleza.

This is kinda hard to explain if you aren't a member
of the cult or you simply don't get it. Señor Frogs is
actually best known in Mexico as a watering hole
where cruisers get so drunk that they dance on tables
and sometimes even miss the boat. Their logo
merchandise is a big deal, if you're in on the party.
I happen to be a fan, so I shop all the stores. My
favorite item is the frog hat, of course.

Foodstuffs

SPICY CARIBBEE
154 Calle del Cristo.

This tiny shop sells mostly spices and cookbooks
and island seasonings and sauces and great cooking
things, but it also has some bath and toiletry items
from the Spicy Caribbee line, which is one of my
favorites.

LUNPOL
Street vendor near Tourist Office.

Luis Polanco sets up his little table and cart and sells
little creations with frogs—San Juan is devoted to
its little frogs—that are dressed in the attire of various professions. Unusual.

Jewelry

BARED & SONS, INC.
264 Calle La Fortaleza.

If you are ready to stop laughing and try a serious source for jewelry as well as china and crystal, go to Bared, which is the kind of place where local brides register. Prices are 10% higher than in St. Thomas, so ask for a discount or hold out. The Lismore wineglass is $27.50 in St. Thomas and everyplace else in the Caribbean; it's $35 here. The store advertises that watches are up to 50% less than in the United States—but be prepared with hometown discounted prices before you get too impressed. The selection of china and crystal upstairs happens to be good; this is one of the best stores in San Juan.

Off-Price

MARSHALL'S
Plaza de Armas.

This is about the worst Marshall's I have ever been to, but it's a branch of the famous off-price store we all love. It's in the heart of the Caribbean, so if you need something, chances are that the prices here are better than elsewhere. Don't knock it. The store has several levels to it and sells men's, women's, and kids' clothing as well as housewares. It's a little claustrophobic when you first walk in, but stick with it, you just might get lucky.

Outlets

RALPH LAUREN / POLO FACTORY STORE
205 Calle del Cristo.

There happens to be about two dozen Ralph Lauren factory outlet stores all over the U.S., and that includes San Juan. Frankly, this is always my first destination when I hit town: Calle del Cristo is the best street in Old San Juan, and there's no reason not to start at the top of the world.

First off, the shop is very nice, almost as nice as a regular Lauren shop. The home furnishings department is upstairs; the women's portion of the store fills what used to be the Christian Dior outlet (if you are an old timer), so it's one half of the downstairs space because the store has been enlarged.

The store sells a small amount of irregulars, but mostly sells sale items that just didn't make it the year, or the season, before. There are no drop-dead bargains on first-quality merchandise; prices are about 25% less than retail. But the prices on irregulars, which are hard to find anywhere, are very good, if you don't mind slightly damaged merchandise. Actually, it's often hard to even find the damage.

I have bought a scad of men's short-sleeve knit polo shirts, in discontinued colors with the labels cut in half to indicate they are damaged, for $20 each. Granted, some of these colors were shades you wouldn't wear outside the Caribbean or the South of France (like turquoise), but a few were sensible hues. The more sensible shirts were $25 per.

The first-quality shirts cost $35 in the outlet, $45 in most Caribbean Polo shops, and $65 in most U.S. department or Polo stores. Prices are identical to those offered in all other Ralph Lauren/Polo outlets, although I find there's a little better selection of Caribbean colors in San Juan. Meanwhile, there were tons of pocket-Ts for $10!

I bought what I'm sure is a one-off: a knit, cream-colored silk Ralph Lauren Couture short sleeve sweater for $59.

The sales help is friendly; the shipping rate is determined not by weight but by how much you spend. If you spend over $300, the shipping is free. Ask.

The store is open 7 days a week; Monday through Saturday 10am to 6pm, Sundays 12 to 5pm.

DOONEY & BOURKE FACTORY STORE
200 Calle del Cristo.

In keeping with the neighborhood, this outlet is also as fancy as the surrounding ones. The store looks like a colonial home, but it is filled with Dooney & Bourke leather goods at discounted prices. This doesn't mean they are cheap, they just cost less than at Saks. More affordable items are kept close to the cashier's desk.

COLE HAAN
204 Calle San Justo.

This one is tricky because the store is actually factory direct, which means that some prices are regular, some are lightly discounted, and only a small portion of the stock is truly at outlet prices (30% to 50% off). Open 7 days a week; shoes and accessories for men and women.

LONDON FOG FACTORY OUTLET STORE
156 Calle del Cristo.

Who cares if you aren't planning on rain during your Caribbean vacation? Buy your bargains, and have them shipped home; then buy a small folding umbrella to keep in your handbag. (It only rains in the Caribbean in the summer and early fall.) There are selections for every member of the family in a series of chambers that interconnect and hold raincoats, ski coats, ready-to-wear, and everything else. Their business card lists all of their other factory outlets (there are about 20 others), so check to see if there's one near your hometown.

Rum

I may not be the world's biggest (or best) drinker, but I love crazy Caribbean rum drinks. And frankly, part of the charm of San Juan is the fact that when you go factory outlet shopping here, the factory makes rum!

Don't forget the best secret about Puerto Rican rum: There is no limit on the amount of rum you can take home because you never left the United States. Get it? While you are in San Juan, especially if you are island-hopping or cruising to several ports, you are in a psychological state that says "vacation" and "foreign" and maybe even "U.S. Customs Allowance."

Of course, each bottle of rum is heavy (and breakable) so you might not want to pack up a suitcase full, and you might not want to carry a case on and off a lot of airplanes. And rum at the most expensive American liquor store is not as expensive as French champagne . . . but still, you can save 30% to 50% on rum when you buy it in Puerto Rico.

There is no such thing as a duty-free liquor store in San Juan, so don't look for one except at the cruise pier. Unless you hit a promotional special, prices everywhere are more or less the same all over the old town. But there are a lot of promotional sales, as various brands battle for your attention and your dollar. Don't forget to check out liquor prices at any of the many **Pueblo** supermarkets.

BACARDI
Route 888, Cataño.

If you take this even more seriously, you'll want to go to the **Bacardi** factory, the world's largest rum distillery. You can go by ferry from Old San Juan, which is more fun than driving there, although there is an overland route as well. The factory is located in Cataño, 15 minutes away.

You get a free tour and a free sample; for tour schedules call ☎ 787/788-1500 or 787/788-8400. Bacardi is closed the last 2 weeks in July and December, and on Sundays (which is, unfortunately, a day that many ships come to town). The factory is open Monday to Saturday, 9 to 10:30am and 12pm–4pm; the tour is free. And *sí, amigo,* you get a free taste. You can also buy booze here.

To get to the factory by boat, head over to Pier 2, Paseo Concepción de Gracia, Old San Juan; the ferry costs $1 round-trip. Once you get off the ferry, there are buses to take you to the factory.

Santons

Santons, or *santos,* are wooden carvings of angels or saints, a specific type of folk art. You'll find them here and there in assorted crafts shops. My best source is Magia.

MAGIA
99 Calle del Cristo.

This workroom-cum-gallery/shop sells the work of many local wood-carvers and I have bought the most soulful of *santos* here, at about $40 each.

OLD SAN JUAN ON A SCHEDULE

. . . .

I am assuming that you are joining your ship in San Juan, have left your luggage on board, and are now off to explore or have come to port for a day's visit and are docked at the main terminal.

As you leave the harbor terminal, you'll spot a pink building, which is the Tourist Information Center. Stop inside and pick up a few maps of the area. From there walk up the hill straight ahead (Calle Tanca) and take a left on Calle La Fortaleza, where you will find most of the popular shops. If you are on a cruise, most of the jewelry stores will have lucky cabin numbers taped outside.

At the end of Calle La Fortaleza, take a right on Calle del Cristo, and head straight to the **Ralph Lauren / Polo Factory Store.** This is a real-live factory outlet, owned by Mr. Lauren himself and one of the authorized stores (he has about two dozen of them across the United States) that sell unsold and imperfect merchandise.

Calle del Cristo has become outlet heaven: Down the street you'll find **Dooney & Burke** as well as **London Fog.** After exhausting your pocketbooks in the outlets, you might want to stop for lunch, or at least coffee, in the famous **Gran Hotel El Convento**

(100 Calle del Cristo). You can dine in the center atrium courtyard and admire your new purchases in an antique setting.

Calle del Cristo also has two good galleries that you might want to visit on your way back down the hill, **Galleria Palomos** and **Galleria Botero.** One block past El Convento and toward El Morro (away from Ralph Lauren) is **Magia,** for *santos,* and a few other artisan's workshops. Do walk the extra block—it's worth it.

Across from Ralph's place, still on Calle del Cristo, are two of the best stores in town: **Pusser's** for beachwear, beach wares (tin cups and more), and wonderful, charming style, and **Spicy Caribbee,** at 154 Calle del Cristo, for Caribbean spices and foods and gifts. The best plantain chips in the Caribbean are sold here—dusted in great spices.

Walk back down Calle La Fortaleza, dropping in at the shops you missed in your rush to get to Ralph Lauren, and head slowly toward the main square, where you can visit real people shops including **Marshall's, Walgreen's,** and even the grocery store.

Finally, head back toward the cruise ship, taking in the local street vendors selling plantain chips and fresh juice, and the craftspeople selling all sorts of silly junk.

Chapter Nine

· · · · · · · ·

THE AMERICAN CARIBBEAN: ST. THOMAS & ST. CROIX

This is a Virgin announcement. It has nothing to do with Richard Branson and Virgin Airways, or Virgin Records, or even Virgin Cola, so please pay attention. There are now *four* U.S. Virgin Islands, each equally placed in the eyes of the law and the Department of the Treasury, which supervises U.S. customs and duties.

Two of the four islands (St. Thomas and St. Croix) have some major shopping sites. While St. Thomas gets most of the hype, the same laws— and the same bargains—apply in all the other islands as well. For more information specific to St. Croix, see page 165.

You're not going to find too much to buy on St. John's, but the laws still apply in terms of liquor or duty-free allowance. Water Island, the newest Virgin, is mainly a residential island, with little shopping to speak of.

WELCOME TO ST. THOMAS

· ·

St. Thomas is one of the four U.S. Virgin Islands, so it is part of the American Caribbean. Unlike Puerto Rico, this is not a commonwealth but a protectorate. Almost every cruise ship calls in Charlotte Amalie, the capital of St. Thomas.

It's not the biggest of the three islands, but it has the biggest rep because it's known as home to the main shopping paradise and largest cruise port in the Caribbean, and is the site of some gorgeous and peaceful resorts. While the main shopping is in downtown Charlotte Amalie, the island is inhabited by locals who don't go around buying crystal and booze every day and who have very real shopping needs.

As a result, you'll find many shopping strips and real people parts to the island. The real people things, by the way, are very expensive—it costs a fortune to live in paradise. If you're just in town for a day via cruise ship, you'll want to be in town shopping. But if you're here for a spell, rent a car and see the island; check out some of the other stores and specialty retailers.

Charlotte Amalie has lost a little of its sparkle, partly because of the hurricane devastation sustained recently. There's been a big turnover in stores with several big names and old favorites seemingly gone forever (Louis Vuitton, Ralph Lauren Factory Store, Java Wraps), but others have moved in, so don't cry for me, Argentina.

Shopping seems to be the lifeblood of the city; your fellow passengers who will snorkle or sunbathe or take Jolly Roger cruises during your week at sea will be all keen and at attention when you get to St. Thomas—they're primed to shop. Many folks come with their own sets of airline wheels so they can snap up tons of booze with an easy spirit.

The shopping scene in St. Thomas sometimes make me a little nervous—it's sort of a feeding frenzy at the local zoo with everyone convinced there are bargains to be had while they madly dash about buying everything in sight. True, there are some serious bargains here—but also some serious fakes and some fancy scams and many of the usual Caribbean retail tactics that make any sensible person stand back and go, "Hey, whoa there, wait a minute."

Charlotte's Web

I have always had the private vision that the license plates on cars in St. Thomas say "Shopper's Paradise" in little letters somewhere, the way the Illinois plate says "Land of Lincoln." Indeed, everyone thinks of this island as the Caribbean shopping mecca.

Charlotte Amalie kind of grows on you. The first time I visited, I shrugged, "Is that all there is?" I was actually hurt and offended that the town was not possessed of what we call "shopping cutes."

Charlotte Amalie isn't half as nice as Bermuda, but it does have a much bigger selection of goods and a lot of choices and categories of merchandise that other islands don't stock up on.

However, Charlotte Amalie is a town that invites you to wander its streets and poke into all its shops. There are people from all over the world here, who sell merchandise from all over the world. All of this hoopla may have been created for tourists, but in the long run, I'm not complaining.

In the main part of town, there is a main street (which is called Main Street even though that's not its name) and there are many passages and streets between streets. Many of the passages have Danish street names, which seem confusing but really are not. To translate, understand that *gade* means street. The word preceding is the name of that street. Norre Gade is North Street and Kongens Gade is Kings Street.

Attention St. Thomas Shoppers

Even though most cruise passengers are waiting for St. Thomas to do their big shopping and even though the U.S. government wants to encourage you to do so through the extra tax-free bonus granted to you, I really think you should be done with a lot of your shopping already. I like to consider St. Thomas as the cherry on top of the sundae.

My thoughts in a nutshell:

- I've bought or will buy all my Ralph Lauren at the factory store in San Juan;
- I've bought my perfumes in a French port of call;
- I've bought electronics and cameras in St. Maarten (10% less expensive than St. Thomas).

That means that all I'm going to consider in St. Thomas is:

- Fakes and faux junk from the stalls selling Fendi-esque suitcases and the like;
- China, crystal, and items that need to be shipped so that I can take advantage of the U.S. Postal Service;
- A Rolex watch (ha!);
- Booze.

Local Prices

Although hype would like you to believe that the best buys and the best prices of the entire Caribbean are in St. Thomas, most insiders will agree that prices are 10% less in St. Maarten. St. Thomas does have much more selection, however.

Also note that in some categories of goods, it's not the price but the quality. Most of the perfumes sold in the U.S. Virgin Islands, even from European brands, come from the North American arm of that fragrance house, which means they are made with denatured alcohol (see page 64 if this is meaningless to you). It doesn't matter what kind of a bargain you get pricewise if what you really wanted was a different product.

Money Matters

As part of the U.S., the Virgin Islands trade in U.S. dollars. Most stores take credit cards.

Play Post Office

Just as in San Juan, you are technically in part of the U.S. and you get to use the U.S. Postal Service. U.S. postal rates are charged (this is good news); the stamps in your wallet can be used on postcards (this is good news), items that you send home are still dutiable (this is news). So watch it, but know the laws: You are allowed $50 a day in unsolicited gifts to the U.S. For shoppers who want to mail packages home, there's a very nice post office right in the heart of town, at Emancipation Square.

Best Buys of St. Thomas

Booze, booze, and more booze. I have no idea how the U.S. Virgin Islands became booze heaven, but the law is that you can export five bottles of liquor plus an additional bottle if it is produced locally. This is not hard as they make rum around just about every corner. I've heard stories of people who came down on a prewedding trip, just to stock up. I've heard tales of young people who come once a year just to stock their home bars.

I don't drink enough to make this my wild card, but two adults can actually between them be schlepping home a dozen bottles! If this is your intention, please make sure that each of your bags has one of those wheel-y things.

I did check my six pack of liquor as luggage once—and it was stolen!

Aside from booze, the most highly touted thing in the area is jewelry. To my eye, the entire shopping district looks like one big Fortunoff's—there's not a lot of classy stuff here. However, if you're into cocktail rings for $99 or cheapie this and that, you may have the time of your life. The real savings are on very expensive top-of-the-line brands and big-name watches, where you can handily save 20% to 25%, if you were planning on spending $10,000 in the first place.

Linens are highly prized by many cruisers looking for a bargain. They are all from the Orient and are competitively priced with discount sources in the U.S. I carry a catalog from Domestications with me (☎ 800/746-2555) so that I can comparison shop. If you have no other chance in your shopping career to buy this kind of thing, it may indeed tickle your fancy. Extremely sophisticated shoppers will not be amused.

Many designer shops are situated in Charlotte Amalie, with prices that are less than Stateside and even Europe. The problem here is that some of these stores are real and some are not, and it's downright confusing. When Louis Vuitton left town, I took that as my clue to avoid big-ticket designer items.

Store Hours

Most stores are open Monday through Saturday 9am to 5pm. Some stores are open on Sundays. Stores will open or extend hours if a lot of ships are in port.

The Lay of the Land

Your ship will more than likely come to the terminal at Havensight, adjacent to the Havensight Mall (gee, how convenient). The main downtown area of Charlotte Amalie will be in front of you, just around the corner from the pier about a mile away, while this is technically walking distance, you really don't want to walk it. Usually, free shuttle buses or pay shuttle buses and/or taxis are waiting at the pier.

Once in town, note that the three main thoroughfares running through town are Waterfront Highway (on the dock side of town), Main Street (Dronningens Gade), and Back Street (Vimmelskaft Gade).

Shops begin on the Tolbod Gade near the Post Office and continue to Market Square. There are over 400 stores between the Post Office and Market

Square. The neighborhood changes drastically at Market Square and becomes a little seedy. The less expensive stores and what I call the fox-trot stores are in this area. Fox-trot stores, by the way, are the ones that you trot right into and trot right out of, after realizing that they sell more of the same old junk.

Between Havensight and downtown, you probably have all the shopping ops you can stand. But if you need to know about more, fear not, see a complete neighborhoods section beginning on page 150.

General Stores R Us

St. Thomas is different from all other ports, especially when it comes to the style laid out for shoppers. Many of the stores in Charlotte Amalie sell a little bit of everything. You've seen this concept already with Little Switzerland stores all over the Caribbean, but the trend is carried to the extreme in Charlotte Amalie.

Some of the stores are such a mishmash of goods that fighting your way through the jungle (of goods and passengers) is worthy of a Number 10 headache.

With prices uniform throughout the island (except where you can bargain on some jewelry items), you can go to one of these general stores, and do it all. Simply pick the one that feels best to you. I've heard that Little Switzerland actually owns **A.H. Riise** as well, so it possibly doesn't matter which store you pick.

I usually end up at A.H. Riise (pronounced *Reese*), but there are others with a seemingly endless supply of goods. Because the stores sell everything, I have changed the way the listings are done in this chapter because if I wrote these items up by category, you'd just see the same old stores again and again.

Also please note that the general stores do have branches at **Havensight Mall** near the cruise terminal, but these stores are smaller and not worthy of your talents. They best serve for last-minute adjustments when you realize you should have bought something more or you forgot to get a gift for the cat sitter.

My best trick is to call a few of the toll-free numbers from the big general stores (numbers are provided in the store listings) and get the catalogs before I leave for my cruise. That way, I can comparison shop in each island as well as on board my ship.

Getting Around

Once you get to downtown Charlotte Amalie, you'll want to walk and walk and walk. And once you get accosted by the insistent cab drivers, who think nothing of pulling up right alongside you and saying, "Taxi?," you'll wish you could walk everywhere on this island.

The situation isn't much better when you are out of town. The resorts have vans that pick up passengers at designated times to take them to the various locations posted on a board. You pay the set price.

There's no such thing as a private cab unless you make special arrangements for one. While it's nice to know that there are set prices and you're not getting ripped off, you are totally stuck with the system; no room for negotiation here. Prices are always per person.

Do note that traffic on St. Thomas moves on "the wrong side of the road."

St. Thomas Neighborhoods

St. Thomas is divided into zones and neighborhoods with all kinds of exotic names, many of which are familiar to you because of advertising from resorts (like Cowpet, Bolongo, and Frenchman's Reef). But the main shopping is in Charlotte Amalie or a nearby area like:

HAVENSIGHT

If you come to St. Thomas via cruise ship, your ship will dock alongside the town of Charlotte Amalie at the piers in the neighborhood of Havensight. While it's walking distance to town, you'll get to the stores much faster in one of those buses (called safari buses) or in a taxi. But don't pass up the Havensight Mall!

SUGAR ESTATE

Just a few yards down the road from Havensight Mall and moving off toward the right is the area called Sugar Estate, which is pretty much a real people part of town. It's going to be your part of town if you are staying in a condo and need a grocery store or a few famous fast-food outlets. There's also a **Woolworth's** in this area. One-day tourists can ignore this neighborhood, but longer-staying visitors may well want to check it out.

CORAL WORLD

Coral World isn't really a neighborhood, but a world unto itself, and a bit of a way out of Charlotte Amalie (a 5- or 10-minute drive). No one in her right mind comes here to shop, but you know us—get a little culture, get a little goodie. There's a souvenir shop, **Pearl Bay,** where your kids will go wild picking up oysters and hunting for pearls, and several little shops in a bazaarlike atmosphere selling area handicrafts and island jewelry. This is a great family outing and a wonderful way to keep the kids happy while you still take in a browse or two.

TUTU

A real people neighborhood, Tutu includes the rather well-known tourist attraction, **Tillet's Garden.** Tillet's Garden is an oasis of jungle and parrots with a villa and some outbuildings. The Tillets

(Mr. and Mrs.) live here and have their studios here; you can buy some of their artwork or their silk-screened fabrics or stop by the potter's shop, etc. There's also a Mexican restaurant. They have a small brochure and a mail-order form; they are most famous for their once-a-year craft show. Ask.

Snack & Shop

LA SCALA
Palm Passage.

There's a coffee bar inside A.H. Riise, and there's a Fat Tuesday if you must have that Jello Shot, but for me, it's La Scala, a nice sit down lunch (alfresco) in the prettiest of the passages and near the fanciest stores. Pasta, of course.

St. Thomas Resources

BOOZE

Know the difference between 750ml (what's called a "fifth") in the States and one litre, which is larger. When you comparison shop, make sure you are comparing the same size bottles.

A.H. RIISE LIQUORS
37 Main St., Charlotte Amalie; Havensight Mall.

Since I do most of my local shopping in A.H. Riise, I also patronize their liquor departments, which I find well stocked. They do have the fancy big names in single malt whiskey at okay prices, which may not actually be much less than what you can find at promotional rates elsewhere. However, they sell Madarine Napoleon Orange Liqueur for $17 per litre, which is a stunning bargain. Go figure. Grand Marnier at $17.50 struck me as an awfully good deal.

You'll do better on more commercial brands; most bottles seem to cost between $10 to $15. The store, like all others, will match any current advertised price from other stores in town or on your ship. They also print up a brochure that's almost like a newsletter; it has coupons in it and details their promotional purchases.

AL COHEN'S DISCOUNT LIQUORS
Across from Havensight.

If you pride yourself on being the kind of shopper who never goes for the obvious, then head over here—you can walk—for more booze bargains. It's a little bit funkier than elsewhere in town, so it's somewhat satisfying if you hate the prepackage tourist approach to local shopping.

BOLERO
Main St., Charlotte Amalie. ☎ *809/776-5200.*

Bolero publishes—as do most of the shops—a price list and tout their specials. Their specialty, however, is prepacks, which they discount by another 10%. So on the pack they call "Rummies Delight" (five bottles of rum), you are given the U.S. price ($53.18), the regular Virgin Islands price ($28.30), and the Bolero price ($25.50). Their ads claim that they will beat all published liquor prices; they print a comparison shopper's price sheet so you can go around town and fill in everyone's price and see for yourself.

SPARKY'S
Main St., Charlotte Amalie.

Sparky's specialty is in really cheap booze. Gin begins at $1.99, Scotch at $2.99, vodka at $1.99. Obviously at these prices, the specialty is not the big brands, but they have those, too. And, after all, not everyone wants or needs top-of-the-line brands. They, too, claim they will beat all published liquor prices.

CAMERAS & ELECTRONICS

ROYAL CARIBBEAN
23 & 33 Main Sts., Havensight Mall.

No, the cruise line doesn't own this shop; it's one of the two better-stocked stores for cameras and electronics. There are two different storefronts on Main Street as well as a shop in the mall next to the pier. They also sell watches and much more. They carry all big names and claim to be the largest supplier of big-name cameras in the Caribbean.

SPARKY'S
Main St.

Sparky's is one of those general store–type places that sells everything, but I once saw such an interesting camera gimmick that I pass it on. Sparky's runs a close-out sale at which they effectively cut out all the local competition on certain advertised items. I think these are models that were being replaced by the makers and would be hard to move without a big promotional sale, but they claimed their close-out prices were 20% to 25% off regular duty-free prices.

CARIBBEAN STYLE

DOWN UNDER TRADERS
Waterfront Hwy.

Virgin Island recipe books plus seafood seasonings, Caribbean mustards, jellies, teas, and spice mixes.

A.H. RIISE
Main St.

I promise not to keep going on and on about this store, which is my main squeeze when I am in town, but they do have what they call Calypso Corner in the store where they sell Caribbean-made souvenirs and foodstuffs and gift items. The Sunny Caribbe line, which I buy everywhere, is sold here at good prices; the soap is $4 per baggie—I have paid $5 in other islands.

LOCAL COLOR
Hibiscus Alley, Charlotte Amalie.

This is an adorable little alley of shops off Main Street, don't miss it. This particular shop has a super photo op out front, but watch those shadows as all our pictures came out dark! The store sells plenty of, well, local color—sportswear in bright shades and hues and prints and patterns. I love the Jams line, which is actually from the U.S. (I think), but you will see it all over the Caribbean (and Florida) and will fall for it if you like color and pattern.

DESIGNERS

Base, Grand Hotel Court

Benetton, Main Street, Charlotte Amalie, and Havensight

Cartier, Main Street

Esprit, Waterfront Highway, Charlotte Amalie

Fendi, Main Street

Gianni Versace, Palm Passage

Gucci, Waterfront Highway

Guy Laroche, Palm Passage, Charlotte Amalie

Louis Feraud, Janine, Palm Passage, Charlotte Amalie

Nicole Miller, Main Street

Ralph Lauren / Polo, Palm Passage

FAKES

There's a street market at Emancipation Square, where the vendors are stocked with tons o'fakes. I bought a Fendi-esque rollerboard for $100 cash that was great fun for wheeling around town and carrying all my packages, but it sustained an injury in the zipper not long after purchase. I was grateful it made it back to New York! Be sure to bargain hard if you want any of this junk, and remember not to buy too many fakes as you still have to go through U.S. Customs and you are not allowed to bring in any fakes that may be for resale.

GENERAL STORES

📑 LITTLE SWITZERLAND
Main St. and Emancipation Sq., Charlotte Amalie; Havensight Mall.

Little Switzerland is one of the most famous names in the Caribbean, with stores on just about every island. They also have a large and glossy catalog and do a big mail-order business. This is rather a one-stop-do-it-all kind of shop, selling just about everything, although the three shops have some different items. The selections in fine china, crystal, and silver here are the main attraction. Prices are the same as in St. Maarten, but remember you have a larger import allowance here.

I adore Little Switzerland, but by the time my ship gets to St. Thomas, I have usually shopped in every Little Switzerland in the Basin and am ready for a slight change of pace. They may also be having a promotional sale, which always makes the heart beat a little faster.

Call for a catalog or for prices before you leave home, ☎ 800/524-2010.

📑 A.H. RIISE GIFT SHOP
37 Main St., Charlotte Amalie.

The main store gets my award as the best of the general stores. The store is large and stocked with all the biggest and best brands in American and European merchandise (yes, even Tiffany & Co.!). The store is even cute, in its old stone warehouse.

There are seemingly many parts to the A.H. Riise Gift Shop Alley, which is a lower-end version of the main store at a different location. The main store is located in a restored 19th-century Danish warehouse. Each department is fully stocked with the finest and most comprehensive lines. It is very impressive.

My best strategy for shopping in Charlotte Amalie, especially if there are a lot of ships in port and the stores are crammed, is to hightail it to Riise first off to do my basic shopping. Then I browse at leisure, but I get here before the crowds, whenever possible.

For catalog or price info call ☎ 800/524-2010 or 800/524-2037.

JEWELRY

Even if you hate jewelry, you'll find yourself drooling after an hour or two in Charlotte Amalie. Everyone seems decked out: The tourists are all wearing "beggar's beads" (shiny and sometimes semiprecious stones strung together in a necklace—$10 to $15); honeymooners all sport $100 Cardow cocktail rings (women do, anyway); and locals are decked out in sterling silver fashion chunks.

There seem to be three kinds of jewelry sold here: Hong Kong cheap, Italian middle class, and the good stuff. Many of the stores sell chains by the foot or yard; I am amused by the shops who almost violate copyright laws when coming dangerously close to someone else's genius—Paloma Picasso and Angela Cummings are both imitated with spectacular results.

The bottom line: Know your stuff, and you'll go home happy; or be thrilled with junk, and keep smiling.

Because I am such a fuddy duddy when it comes to jewelry, I have to remind you that serious money and serious stuff deserves serious thought and a store with a serious reputation. If you are going to spend big bucks and do something big time, go with either **H. Stern** or **Amsterdam & Sauer,** or one of the name brands from the official dealers such as Tiffany at **Riise** or Rolex at **Little Switzerland.**

See page 21 for more on buying jewelry in the Caribbean. Note that all the general stores in St. Thomas sell jewelry and watches.

AMSTERDAM SAUER
14 Main St., Charlotte Amalie; Havensight Mall.

Amsterdam Sauer is a Brazilian jeweler; they aren't as large or as famous as H. Stern but they are as trustworthy and are highly competitive. The stores are all over Brazil but are otherwise not represented in the Caribbean except in St. Thomas. There are New York offices to help you with guarantees and consumer questions and returns; customer service is toll free in the U.S., ☎ 800/345-3564.

Because the firm is Brazilian, their specialty is colored gemstones.

CARDOW JEWELERS
Main St., Charlotte Amalie.

If you ever wished for a supermarket for jewelry, this is it. Affordable jewelry for everyone is here at Cardow Jewelers. There are items in every price range and for every buyer, divided into every category, and clearly marked with large signs.

I get frightened in this store, although I admit that while it's not sophisticated, it can be lots of fun. With much of the sparkle going for $99 and less, the idea that you can afford so many pretty things makes the adventure of shopping fun. The jewelry is organized according to type and price range. The sales help never seems to tire of pulling out the trays.

CARTIER
Palm Passage at Main St., Charlotte Amalie.

Located at the forefront of Palm Passage, Cartier is a small and selective shop. The selections are not extensive. There is some jewelry, lighters, leather, and pens. The most shocking thing about the store is that all the stock is piled up in the windows. You must really know what you want (or see it in a window) in order to get helpful service. The staff is decidedly cool and encourages serious shoppers only.

COLOMBIAN EMERALDS INTERNATIONAL
Main St., Charlotte Amalie.

You have to be impressed with these guys; they have large fancy stores all over the Caribbean and have even moved into Alaska to catch more of the cruise business. What they are are simply marketing geniuses; they know what the majority of cruise passengers want and how much they want to spend, and they have a knack for getting it right. Frankly, I wouldn't make any big purchase, especially of emeralds, but if you just wanna have some fun, come on down.

Yes, they sell other gemstones and jewelry items besides emeralds.

DI/ DIAMONDS INTERNATIONAL
3A Main St. and 31 Main St., Charlotte Amalie.

Specialists in unset diamonds; customer service offered in New York. Call ☎ 800/444-4025 (in St. Thomas) or 800/434-8784 (in the U.S.) for information, prices or customer needs.

H. STERN
Main St., Charlotte Amalie; Havensight Mall.

Three stores on Main Street and another at Havensight, H. Stern is considered the most trusted jeweler in the Caribbean. I happen to be a personal friend of Hans Stern, so maybe I am not objective here, but I've known him for well over a dozen years and have learned a good bit of what I know about jewelry and jewelry stores from him. Hans is retired now, and his sons run the business; they have brought in some new and younger looks to spark things up. (You haven't shopped until you see the rings with the stars etched inside the golden bands of the rings!)

Like most big-time retailers in St. Thomas, H. Stern has several locations. But most interestingly, the two main stores in Charlotte Amalie are very different from each other. One store (12 Main St.) is a very nice, but rather traditional, jewelry store, where you can get anything.

The other store is the winner. It carries more fashionable merchandise, and is one of the nicest renovations in town—old stone walls and clean white wood create a rich, elegant, and very chic feeling. There is more of an emphasis on strict quality at H. Stern than at some other jewelers in town. Everything is good, well crafted, heavy, and pricey. Although prices are cheaper in St. Thomas than for comparable merchandise in the United States, we are still talking top-of-the-line here.

There is a sale nook of markdown items upstairs; there's a nice bathroom here as well. The third shop sells watches.

For prices or more information or consumer information, call ☎ 800/524-2024. You may return an item up to 1 year after purchase. Oh yes, and you get miles through American Airlines even for purchases made with cash!

LEATHER GOODS

Most of the many handbags for sale come in from the Orient and are the latest in eelskin fashions. I happen to loathe eelskin. The European imports may prove pricey. If you are buying Gucci, compare prices on your ship to those in town, but the Gucci prices are pretty good here.

COACH
Main St.

New kid on the block, sort of discounted like at airports and duty free. A good buy.

FENDI
Main St.

How can I tell this is a real Fendi shop? Simple! The prices are outrageously high! Wait for Italy!

GUCCI
Waterfront Hwy.

I wish I could truly explain this to you, but this is not a real Gucci store. It's just some sort of legal finagle that approximates Gucci—like all the other Gucci stores in Mexico and the Caribbean. It's not against the law, mind you, but this stuff was not designed by Tom Ford and is not what's sold in New York or Italy for that matter. Goods cannot be returned in the U.S. nor repaired by a real Gucci.

The store is in an old house, most easily reached from the water side on Waterfront Highway.

THE LEATHER SHOP
Main St. & Havensight.

I went into this store because the windows said they sold Bottega Veneta and I wanted a bargain, but no luck there. There was a Fendi sale in progress and I bought a tote bag at a great price, but mostly I found the price system confusing and couldn't tell if there were serious bargains or not. The store sells a lot of luggage and if you need luggage because you bought too much, this is your source, but I didn't find the prices to be dirt cheap. Still, they feature good brands and there is no fear of fakes.

LINENS

OMNI LINEN
Raadets Gade, between Burger King and Main St.

The store is a little bit behind the others (hence the specific address), but they import directly from Hong Kong and sell many a tablecloth for $25 or less.

MR. TABLECLOTH
6 Main St., Charlotte Amalie.

Much Hong Kong merchandise, but plenty of low prices, especially when compared to the U.S. You will not find country or Provençal styles anywhere, as in Bermuda. Look for the usual in embroidered, cut and drawn, crocheted, etc. If prices seem incredibly cheap, ask if the work is handmade or machine made.

MALLS & SHOPPING CENTERS

There really aren't any malls in St. Thomas like the ones in the United States. There are strips and small shopping centers and even passages, but few real malls—even though some retailers may band together and call their collection of shops a mall.

Royal Dane Mall   Royal Dane Mall is actually a federation of 23 stores encompassing three alleys with one entrance on Main Street and three more entrances on Waterfront Highway. Check out, among others, **Portico,** for the chic stuff in women's ready-to-wear.

Havensight Mall   Imagine our delight when our cruise ship parked itself next door to a mall. This is actually a series of stucco-and-wood strips, with various numbers and signs with fingers that point this way and that. Almost all the major stores have a branch here, and the atmosphere is extremely pretty and reminds one of California. If you're departing from St. Thomas on an extended cruise, note that there is a supermarket here (small) that has soft drinks and snacks and foods you can stock your cabin with.

The mall was developed by the West India Trading Company, which sounds romantic and swashbuckling to me. These people were into shopping even before us. Furthermore, Havensight is all air-conditioned (as is most of downtown) and a lot more charming than regular old Charlotte Amalie. The stores aren't as big as those in town, but you can go broke here just the same. There are 5 strips, with a total of about 35 to 40 stores. Believe me, if you don't even go into downtown because you hate crowds and you hate to shop (shame on you), you can do just fine right here. Yes, there is a **Gucci** shop.

Grand Hotel Court   It's a mall not a hotel; stores include a good news agent, **Irmela's,** which is a local icon for pearls and jewelry; **Base,** and a few others as well. Near Emancipation Square.

MARKETS

Hmmm, well, this isn't a town for great markets or even decent markets, but there are two markets that you should know about and they may catch your fancy. They're at either end of the main shopping district of downtown Charlotte Amalie.

Market Square is the pavilion where slaves were once sold, on the far end of town. Now there are tables there and local farmers, honey makers, and the like sell homemade and homegrown goodies. Sort of funky but not the best of this sort of thing you've ever seen.

Emancipation Square, also called Emancipation Park, has a square alongside it that is sometimes called Vendor's Square. This is filled with stalls selling fake designer leather goods and touristy items, like caps with Rasta curls attached, and more.

OUTLETS

PUSSER'S CLOSEOUT STORE
Across from Havensight.

You won't need a real street address, but then again, if the stock doesn't improve by the time you get here, you won't need this address either. As much as I adore Pusser in San Juan, and appreciate it in St. Thomas, the outlet store isn't great. But it's open on Sundays, 10am to 4pm!

PERFUME

In St. Thomas, most perfumes are bought through the big general stores. A few of these stores carry an exclusive line, but for the most part, all brands, American and European, are available. Discounts vary with the brand, American brands are only discounted about 10%.

TROPICANA
Main St.

If you prefer to shop in a store that devotes all its energy and expertise to fragrance and perfume, Tropicana has tons of fragrance and many of the big brands in makeup and beauty treatments.

Charlotte Amalie: Shop, Shop & Ship Tour

Those who have been cooped up on a cruise ship, forced to enjoy the sun, pool, games, nightlife, and good food . . . suffer no more. You have landed in shoppers' paradise. As you get off the ship, you are immediately hit with a shopping center. The Havensight Mall has gathered together many of the major retailers, who have opened satellite stores here, just for the cruise traffic. You can do all your shopping and be back on the ship in a matter of hours. Prices are the same as in town. You will find more selection in the town shops, but it is less hectic at the mall.

I actually suggest a quick tour of the Havensight Mall and then a taxi into town. If you can't find what you need in town, you will at least know if it is available at Havensight Mall. My personal method is to head directly to A.H. Riise and then cut back and tour the town. If you prefer to do this in a more rational way, begin your tour at the Post Office and Emancipation Square, where there's a flea market selling mostly fake designer stuff.

Across the street is one of the branches of Little Switzerland, and then in half a block, you will be on the Main Street (Dronningens Gade). Walk away from the Post Office, and stop in at **Cardow, Rosenthal, Tropicana, Little Switzerland,** and **A.H. Riise.**

Now you're cookin'—A.H. Riise Gift Shop Alley. Shop 'til you drop; and no, you do not have to schlep all that stuff with you all day; they will send your booze purchases directly to the ship for you.

You will have done a major amount of shopping at this point, but will not have been even halfway through town. Walk back up the alley to Main Street, turn left, and stop in at **A.H. Riise Liquors, Royal Caribbean, H. Stern,** and **Boolchand's.**

You will now have visited most of the biggies. Wander down Main Street, looking into the various alleys along the way. They each have some little find that is worth discovering. Palm Passage is the designer alley, and you'll know you're there when you reach **Cartier.**

Walk down Palm Passage, enjoying the designer wares, and take a left on Waterfront. This is also a shopping street, but less congested with stores and more congested with restaurants. You will even find **Kentucky Fried Chicken** and **McDonald's.**

WELCOME TO ST. CROIX
. . . .

St. Croix is the largest of the four Virgin Islands, and while it's not the most famous shopping destination, the island has done a tremendous amount of rebuilding since its hurricane devastation, and things are looking awfully good. Several ships are now offering St. Croix, rather than St. Thomas, in order to give you a slightly different experience, and there are some ships that offer both!

St. Croix has two cute little shopping cities, so hotels and resorts are going in for the kill: Frederiksted still doesn't have that much to blow your socks off, but new little shopping strips are opening. And Christiansted is expanding like mad.

Getting There

You can reach St. Croix via the many major airlines, or by ferry or seaplane from St. Thomas. Note that St. Croix is not the kind of place you go for a day trip from St. Thomas, especially if you are a shopper. St. Croix is best enjoyed from a resort or as a cruise port.

Money Matters

Despite its Danish past, St. Croix, like St. Thomas, is part of the United States, and the dollar is king.

Annual Events

Each March, the **Whim Plantation** holds what they call the Antiques Furniture Auction as part of the West Indies Symposium. This event is such a big deal that designers fly in from all over the world (any excuse to see sun in March, no doubt). We are talking large pieces of furniture with price tags usually over $1,000. Most of the furniture comes form old mills and plantations; some has been damaged by time and hurricanes.

Many of the antique pieces are damaged but can be repaired once you get them home or repaired locally before shipping. There are experts on hand to help with restorations and shipping. For more info, call the Tourist Office (☎ 800/372-8784).

St. Croix Neighborhoods

CHRISTIANSTED

Christiansted is one of two main cities (both ports where cruise ships dutifully deposit day-trippers) on the island. It's the larger of the two, the more colorful, and the best possibility for the shopper, although this is not big-time shopping on the same scale as Charlotte Amalie or many of the other port cities.

The town was created with bricks that came back as ballast on sugar ships (the sugar went out, the bricks came back in) and has that old-fashioned feeling that one would expect of a village that has flown seven different nations' flags. Shops may carry very expensive merchandise, yet look very unimpressive to the naked eye. Many stores are of the general-store type—they sell some of anything or a little of everything. Liquor stores abound because of the duty allowance.

Cruise ships come to port at Gallows Bay.

FREDERIKSTED

Not to be written off as merely a sleepy little village, this sleepy little village (16 miles from Christiansted) has a tremendous amount of charm, some cute inns, and several shops worth browsing. Get-up-and-go types will want to take in both cities on a day in port. Cruise ships dock at the end of a new pier that leads right to town.

AIRPORT

Alexander Hamilton Airport (yes, Hamilton was from this island) is just about in the middle of the two port cities, although it is a little bit closer to Frederiksted. Airport shopping is all but nonexistent. Buy your liquor before you get to the airport!

CARAMBOLA

Carambola is the name of a resort, not a neighborhood, and it is reopened and back among the living. Carambola is almost directly across the island from the airport, on the north side, and is therefore slightly closer to Frederiksted than Christiansted. But you can really do all the shopping you want right there at the resort. There is a lovely gift shop, which sells not only the usual tourist needs like suntan oil and magazines but a lot of designer clothes.

The Rum Game

Cruzan Rum has a distillery in St. Croix (on West Airport Road in Fredriksted) and will give you a tour and a free sample. Call ☎ 800/225-3699 from the mainland for more information. Aside from the tour of the plant, there's a tasting bar in the new pavilion and a drink of the day is served as a freebie. The factory is open to visitors Monday through Friday from 9 to 11:30am and 1 to 4pm.

St. Croix Resources

BOOKS

WRITER'S BLOCK
36C Strand St., Christiansted.

Books, maps, prints, and more.

BOOZE

PAN AM LIQUORS
Pan Am Pavilion, Christiansted.

Although there are scads of general stores and stores that sell liquor, and your ship also has good prices, this shop is conveniently located in the Pan Am Pavilion—*primo* retailing real estate—and gets good marks for shopping cutes. Delivery is free; there is a tasting bar.

CARIB CELLARS
53 King St., Christiansted.

Designed like an old wine cellar, the store wants to be known as the one with the best prices in town. There's a list of specials posted; they are competing for your dollar and want your business.

CARIBBEAN STYLE

JAVA WRAPS
Strand/King Sts., Christiansted.

Brightly colored cotton batiks in fabrics and clothes make this the perfect resort shop; they are made locally by a designer named Twila Wilson, who sustained losses during the worst of the hurricanes but has hung on. I vote this one of the best sources in the Basin.

Note that Java Wraps fabrics can be coordinated with Souleiado and Porthault for a stunning, and very sophisticated, summer look.

The twice-a-year sales are so famous that locals stand in line with tourists.

THE ROYAL POINCIANA
38 Strand St., Christiansted.

A Caribbean spice shop that is unusual and special and not anything like what we've got at home. If you don't need to stock up on Arawak Love Potion, you must need some of Marge's Ginger Garlic relish? You can even get a spice necklace to ward off evil spirits.

GENERAL STORES

VIOLETTE
38 Strand St., Christiansted.

Ladies' ready-to-wear is upstairs; downstairs for Gucci, Cartier, and big-name pens, watches, and more. The Gucci sold here is from the Gucci accessory line, which is different from the Italian Gucci line. Perfume, cosmetics, brand names.

This is part of the Caravelle Arcade, so other stores also have this street address—don't panic.

🛍 LITTLE SWITZERLAND
56 King St., Christiansted.

It just wouldn't be the Caribbean without a branch of Little Switzerland. This is one-stop shopping for just about anyone who wants Aynsley, Fitz & Floyd, Royal Doulton, Villeroy & Boch, Wedgwood, Lalique, Orrefors, Lladro, and more sold from the two-level store, which is well stocked and easy to shop. The store is deep, and the selection excellent.

JEWELRY

COLOMBIAN EMERALDS
Queen Cross St., Christiansted; Strand St., Frederiksted.

Another branch of the store that specializes in those pretty green rocks but also sells other precious stones and watches and jewelry. Chains are sold at a flat price per yard.

OUTLETS

🛍 RALPH LAUREN / POLO FACTORY STORE
52C Company St., Christiansted.

Relocated from St. Thomas, for those of you who remember there was a Ralph outlet in Charlotte Amalie. This is the real thing, although I think the one in San Juan is better. They are different enough that you can shop them both and still have fun.

Chapter Ten

. . . .

THE FRENCH CARIBBEAN: MARTINIQUE, ST. MARTIN/ ST. MAARTEN & ST. BARTS

MARTINIQUE

. . . .

Martinique is possibly the most unusual island in the Caribbean. It doesn't even seem to be in the Caribbean. The port city of Fort-de-France is so French, so much like a city on the Riviera, so full of hustle and bustle, that you must think for a minute to remember where you are. I have had "Nice" moments and flashbacks while on the streets of downtown.

The island itself is also unusual in that it has gray sand (volcanic ash mixed with the sand), junglelike rain forests, and lots of atmosphere. It's also nice to hear everyone speak French. And I mean *really* speak French; this isn't like some of the other islands where French is spoken; here, you do best if you speak some French.

Fort-de-France does not look like New Orleans, nor does it look much—or feel at all—like Marigot, the French city in St. Martin. Marigot is a sleepy little town compared to Fort-de-France; Fort-de-France isn't quite Nice, but it sure vibrates with business of its own. It's not the kind of place where everything stops when the cruise ships come to town, or where street urchins shove tortoise shells in your face or beg you to buy *chiclee* nuts, from which gum is made. Business goes on as usual, and business must be very good. Fort-de-France does not feel like a resort at all, and that really is the main point.

The Shopping Scene

The surprise of Martinique is that you didn't come to shop. Maybe you've heard of **Roger Albert** (considered the most famous perfume shop in the Caribbean Basin) and knew about being able to buy genuine French perfumes, but you probably don't even have your shopping legs yet.

The last time I cruised to Martinique, it was the very first stop we made and I was not psychologically ready to get down and get serious. If you are a Francophile, you quite possibly aren't ready for the jam-packed shopping experience you'll have to cram into your day here—if you are lucky enough to have a day.

You see, many ships, en route to Barbados, must cut short their time in Fort-de-France in order to get on with it, leaving you with only the promise to return to fill another market *panier* (basket). With stores closing for lunch and an early departure time, my, how time flies!

Downtown Fort-de-France, a short taxi ride from the pier, is a spill of tiny narrow streets, Caribbean colors, French colonial architecture (reminiscent of New Orleans), and old-fashioned French stuff painted with local color: locals selling fruits and veggies and *chiclee* from brightly colored plastic wash basins and laundry baskets, people dressed in crazy mismatched colors, neon storefronts alongside rust and decay and too much Caribe—and yet inside, almost hidden, lies some of the bounty of France.

Granted, you didn't come to the Caribbean to do some catalog shopping, but there's something so reassuring about seeing the storefronts for **3Suisses** and **La Redoute,** the two major French catalogs, that you just have to smile and murmur, Lafayette, we have arrived.

Other French chains include everything from the cheapie shoe kingdom **Bata** (my travel companion Mary Jo bought a lovely pair of lace sneakers for $30 there) to **Yves Rocher** (26 rue Blenac) to **Tati** (*mais oui!*) and **Galeries Lafayette.**

The lack of perfection in downtown Fort-de-France reminds you that you are indeed in the Caribbean. The area feels authentic in an unprecedented manner—people actually live and work here, France is doing business here, and you are merely watching. And shopping.

Money Matters

Because Martinique is a part of France (and a very active part of France), the franc is the accepted monetary unit. If you bring francs with you, you might be happier. Of course, credit cards give the best rate of exchange, and there are unusual duty-free and discount laws on this island, so *do not* change too much money into francs, especially if you don't travel to the French Caribbean or *la belle France* on a regular basis.

Taxi rates from the pier to town are fixed and are charged in U.S. dollars. If you try to pay in francs, you'll be at a disadvantage!

Détaxe & French Prices

Prices on most goods in Fort-de-France appear to be much higher than in other Caribbean ports. But wait, it can be explained! It's because French law requires that the total price, including taxes, be posted. However, if an item is for export, a 20% refund is given.

But beware, the refund is only given in so called duty-free shops, and there are only a handful of duty-free shops in Fort-de-France.

Let me emphasize: *There are only a few shops in Fort-de-France, out of the many hundreds there, that are worthwhile to shop in.* So despite the many choices for browsing, there are very few stores where you should shop, and even fewer shops offer really good bargains. In fact, if the dollar is weak, there may be no bargains whatsoever. But then, we are talking about being able to go to a French pharmacy and to even visit a branch of **Tati**, so you will not suffer for lack of amusements.

Détaxe & Discounts

While everyone in France uses the word *détaxe* readily and easily and American tourists have come to know how to get this discount, the *détaxe* in Martinique is rarely called *détaxe* and is considered a simple export discount. The system is a little complicated, so here goes:

- TVA in France is 20.6%, but in Martinique it is 9%;
- The export discount can only be given to those who can prove they are foreigners. In Europe you show your passport as proof and then show your goods to the customs agent as you exit. In Martinique, you only get the export discount (9%) if you pay for goods with a credit card, traveler's checks, or personal checks—all forms of payment that identify you as a foreigner. Cash, even if you show your passport, does not meet the legal requirements.
- If you read in advertisements or guidebooks that certain stores offer a 20% discount for the use of traveler's checks or credit cards, please understand: This is a flat 20% discount that is actually 9% *détaxe plus 11% actual*

discount; it is not a 20% discount on the cost of the goods.

The prices in Martinique are at least 20% higher than anywhere else, even on imported French merchandise. With the discount, the price will be competitive with other islands, or maybe $1 to $2 less expensive.

Some retail stores in Martinique are not "duty free," but they do have promotional sales for visitors during which the discount is (how did you guess?) 20%.

You only get the 20% discount at certain stores, so don't expect to shop anyplace and get money back. Ask before you buy. When the dollar is strong, you might not care. But when the dollar is weak, there aren't enough bargains to go around.

Arriving in Martinique

There are relatively new shopping facilities at the pier in Fort-de-France. There's a little strip center, for lack of a better word, with three or four shops; these shops sell everything you could need including perfumes, French wines and booze, cigars, and even soft drinks and ice. The idea is that if you're going on a shore excursion or you want a tour of the island, you shouldn't have to go into town, you can just load up at the pier.

While the shops here are nice enough and may fulfill your needs, I beg to disagree with the basic premise. You need to go to town!

There's no question that the cutest looking storefront on the island, and possibly in all of the Caribbean, is at the Fort-de-France pier, **La Maison Créole**. Bring your camera. The pier branch of this store is actually better than the downtown branch, but the store still doesn't stock the range of perfumes and beauty goods that Roger Albert carries.

I must also warn you to buy expensive designer items with care and only from a reputable dealer who can be trusted. I saw some things in one of the stores at the pier that were just terrifying; I would be sick to think you got cheated.

Shopping Hours

Stores open at 9am; many of them close for lunch at 1pm and reopen at 3pm. They stay open until 6pm. The market at La Savane begins to set up around 8:30am and is in full swing by 9am.

Because you are now absorbed in a French culture, remember that most stores close for *midi* (mid-day lunch break). Not all of them close, but many do. Remember that often on Saturday the stores close for the day at noon.

There is very little shopping on Sunday, except for pharmacies and a few bakeries and food shops because French law is not keen on Sunday shopping.

The Lay of the Land

The pier is a 5-minute walk from downtown, but it's not an attractive walk and access is difficult because of the highway. The route is considered dangerous to walk by some. A new pier is planned although the pier area has already been enhanced with a nice little shopping facility. There are taxis to take you into town.

The main town square is La Savane, a green park that borders the water on one side and has an L-shape with stores on two other sides. The L-prong coming away from the water has tourist stores; the other half of the L is strictly for real people.

While the area beside the Savane is jam-packed with stores that are sort of rumble-tumble, Caribbean-Riviera-fun style, most of these stores do not offer *détaxe*. Shoppers must decide if they want to look everywhere just for the fun of it; shop the French things just for the frog of it; or hit the duty-free stores and then head for the black sands, the rainforest, the museums, the volcano, or the gourmet dining.

Getting Around

Once you are in town, you can walk everywhere, as the stores are densely packed within a few blocks. If you want to get away from it all, you can take the ferry across the street from La Savane to the Hotel Meridien (make sure you are on the right ferry; there are two). You get a very nice ride across the bay for not much money, and still have the opportunity to do a little shopping at the Meridien. You will need francs to pay for the ferry.

Martinique Neighborhoods

SAVANE

The downtown, central part of Fort-de-France is where the main shopping is done; La Savane is the main square. The farther away from La Savane you get, the more real the stores—and the customers.

BACK STREETS RÉPUBLIQUE

The rue de la République (there seems to be one in every city in France and one on every French Caribbean island) is the main drag for real people shopping in Fort-de-France. It is several blocks back into the grid of streets that make up downtown, and while it's not fancy, it's very funky and picturesque and a little quaint and seedy and sweet. I love this part of town because it validates that I am real and that I have escaped everything fake about a cruise or rich Americans.

THE GRID

Downtown Fort-de-France is laid out on a simple grid system with water on the western edge and La Savane on the southern edge. The rue Victor Hugo is the biggest (not wide, just big in terms of volume and scope) street but all the streets in the grid are fun and packed with Frenchified Caribbean real people stores. Just wander! Check out rue Blénac, rue Antoine Siger, rue Lamartine, and rue Schoelcher. The farthest street on the grid is blvd. Alfassa, which runs along the water. There's some shopping here, too, as well as the tourist office, the ferry piers, and the piers where ships use anchor rather than dock.

MARINA

This is a ferry ride away from Fort-de-France and may not be on your docket. Two of the biggest and best resorts (Boukara and Meridien) share a marina where boats can dock and where there are a few shops. A ferry comes from Fort-de-France to the marina every half hour. If you don't speak French, you might feel intimidated, but the journey is quite straightforward.

As you enter the pier, there are large signs in French and English to direct you. The boat arrives, you get on, you buy your ticket on board. Leaving town is very picturesque, and approaching the Meridien is also nice, although the approach and the idea of the whole thing is more glam than what's become of this particular property. Still, you're here, you're on the water again, life is grand.

Flying fish jump around the boat, windsurfers glide by, and expensive sailboats are docked around you. The marina is marked for the various hotels; go to the Meridien if you want to shop the Roger Albert branch store in the lobby there.

The Marina Shopping Center is simply a group of stores around and behind the marina—nothing to make a special trip for, but nice if you can't get into town from your hotel. **Bleu Caraibe** sells sunglasses and hammocks; **Caribea** sells T-shirts, dolls, and souvenirs; **West Indian Sea Cotton** has hand-painted beach wraps. The best of the bunch is **Citron Vert,** which has two sides. One sells T-shirts, hats, and bags, and the other sells Caribbean art and handicrafts in luscious colors.

Landlubber's Delight

HABITATION LAGRANGE
97225 Le Marigot. ☎ *800/633-7411 in the U.S., or 596/53-60-60.*

Hidden and private and expensive and French Caribbean colonial; go for lunch (see below). Rooms are about $400 per night in season but breakfast is included.

HOTEL BAKOUA-SOFITEL
Pointe du Bout, Trois Ilets. ☎ *800/221-4542, or 596/66-02-02.*

In the "Neighborhoods" section I mentioned the part of town across the bay with the ferry, right? This is the leading hotel over there, where the rich and famous and French and celebrated stay. Topless. Rates range from $200 to $400 per night depending on the room and the season. There's a good restaurant if you just want to make an excursion out of it—it's called Chateaubriand.

Open-Air Markets

La Savane   A series of covered pavilions zigs and zags over terra-cotta tiles in the front portion of La Savane. In this area, both under the roofs and in the open air, vendors set up tables and booths and display their crafts. While most of the items are handmade, some are not. There are even old ladies who sell Coca-Cola from coolers (at a small markup, of course). The atmosphere is fun and colorful; there is a ton of merchandise. Many prices are in dollars.

Several of the vendors sell clothing or items made out of madras, the local plaid fabric associated with Martinique style.

There's a group of telephones at the market; you can use your France Telecom card here to call anywhere in the world.

Marché rue Perrinon   This is much more of a real people market, with its hair ribbons, records, fake "NL" bags meant to imitate "LV" bags, Dark & Lovely hair products, sandals, earrings, and more. It's rather colorful and fun and is a good place to fill out any needs you might have while you are traveling. Francs only.

SHOPPERS BEWARE

The are several stores in town that bear names of big-name designers, and when you read about these stores in tourist magazines, you begin to get sweaty palms and dry teeth. Stay calm. Very, very few of them are franchises. There are stores called Valentino, Chloe, and Au Printemps that are not related to other places or stores of the same name. While there is a legitimate branch of the French department store Galeries Lafayette, Au Printemps is not a branch of the one in France.

SNACK & SHOP

🛍 HABITATION LAGRANGE
97225 Le Marigot. ☎ *596/53-60-60.*

If you have time and the inclination to leave the shopping for a while, taxi to this hillside retreat and find yourself buried in the real Caribbean—a plantation-turned-restaurant, which is also the fanciest inn in town. You don't need to sleep over, just dine alfresco at about $50 per person for a gourmet French fixed-price meal. Reserve if you can and make sure your taxi knows when to return or call a taxi (☎ 596/63-52-78, or 596/71-43-32) before you order coffee so you don't miss your cruise ship.

 ### LINA'S CAFE
15 rue Victor Hugo, Fort-de-France.

Adorable, upscale sort of snack and sandwich shop for a quick bite of français, and more time to shop. Everything from salads to tropical fruit drinks to the French version of American brownies (mmmm . . .) to turkey and cheese sandwiches. They are open from 8am until 11pm except for Monday evenings; closed all day on Sunday.

McDONALD'S
Rue Victor Hugo.

It's McDo in French and yes, they have *frites.*

Martinique Resources

BOOZE

HABITATION CLÉMENT
St. François.

It's a rum distillery with tastings, of course.

LA CASE A RHUM
5 rue de la Liberté, Fort-de-France.

They claim to have the largest selection of rum in the Caribbean Basin. Also own the TTs (tourist traps) called **Tilo** for T-shirts, madras, souvenirs, and the usual suspects. And yes, if you came by plane, they have a shop in the airport, too, so you can get your rum on the fly. They are open every day of the week from 8am to 6pm, which sure makes it easy to shop here.

CARIBBEAN STYLE

COCO CADEAUX
18 rue Blenac, Fort-de-France.

I'm not really certain why I love this shop, but it's got a rumble-tumble rusty-dusty feel to it that takes away from the fact that it's a TT and makes you feel as though you've stepped into another time and place. It sells Haitian art, the usual woodies, and extra amounts of kitsch. Yummy.

ENTRE DES METIERS D'ART
Rue Ernest Deproge, Fort-de-France.

This is a two-part property with a bar for a beer or snack called Coco Loco and a TT that sells mostly wooden items. There is a good selection of local cookbooks (English as well as French) and books on the local fruits and vegetables, which are quite exotic.

GALERIE D'ART
89 rue Victor Hugo, Fort-de-France.

Native craftiness and paintings.

CLEOPATRE
72 rue Victor Hugo, Fort-de-France.

Francophiles who know the French chain of cheap jewelry shops should not be confused; this is more of a nice TT with hand-carved wooden items and local crafts.

AW AN NOU
Corner of rue Victor Hugo and rue Victor Schoelcher.

One of my favorite wooden TTs because there's light, there's lots of room, it's easy to see and shop, and everyone is friendly. Scads of woodens.

TAM TAM
60 rue Victor Hugo.

Wooden shop, 25F for napkin holder, not too cluttered, sort of classy for this type of thing. Great introduction to the look.

DEPARTMENT STORES

GALERIES LAFAYETTE
10 rue Victor Schoelcher.

You won't be transported to the blvd. Haussmann, but this store has some stylist items, some fair prices, a little of everything you might want or need, a little French flair, and a solid discount plan. Show your passport when you pay and *voilà,* 20% discount!

TATI
33 rue de la République, Fort-de-France.

I thought I would fall off the curb when I saw the traditional pink-and-white herringbone Tati awnings with the big violet letters spelling Tati. For those who aren't familiar with this icon, Tati is a discounter with a zillion stores in Paris and a few other stores dotted around France and the provinces. They sell junk with a few gems thrown in so that everyone who is anyone admits to shopping here for a bargain. It's even fun in the Caribbean, if you know what to expect and you aren't expecting Yves Saint Laurent.

MATCH
75 rue Lamartine, Fort-de-France.

There are French *hypermarchés* in Martinique, but they are not in Fort-de-France, and your dedication is probably not so extreme that you want to taxi to one. Therefore you can make do with this small grocery store-cum-dry goods department store that sells French products, much like what you'd expect to find in a larger French *hypermarché*. Also good for le snack or just stocking up your cabin, for personal needs (diapers?), and cheapie beach supplies.

HOME STYLE

 ### GINGER
25 rue Victor Hugo, Fort-de-France.

One of my favorite shops in all the Caribbean, this store is actually divided into two parts in a tiny arcade on the main shopping street. The specialty of the house is the eye of the buyer, who mixes southern Provençale fabrics and a few products with Caribbean hand-painted tiny stucco cottages, flying model airplanes made out of Coca-Cola cans, dishes, candles encrusted with cinnamon and seashells, and scads of goods in azure blue.

CADET DANIEL
72 rue Antoine Siger.

It's a duty free! Lovely place settings, all the china and crystal from the French biggies that you can stand, and prices are excellent—they are also the same as Roger Albert's. The store is over 100 years old and is responsible for setting the most famous tables on the island. They also sell jewelry and souvenir items. Good news: They do not close for lunch.

MUSIC

NUGGET
55 rue Lamartine.

Medium-size music stores where you can buy CDs and tapes, including all the zouk you need. A section marked "Français" sells my beloved Johnny Hallyday—two-CD set, 240F. Da doo ran ran.

PERFUME

ROGER ALBERT
7 rue Victor Hugo.

I don't want to give the impression Fort-de-France is a one-horse town, or a one-store town. But, when it comes to buying perfume or makeup or French luxury goods, it is.

Roger Albert is the undisputed King of the Duty Frees. While there are branch stores dotted around the island in various suburban shopping malls and hotel lobbies, the La Savane shop is a must for every visitor. As a result, especially when a cruise ship comes to port, there can be a mob scene at the counters. Go early!

The reason you shop here is twofold: selection (undisputedly the best in the Caribbean) and trust— you know exactly what you are getting, and you know it's French not North American from a French firm.

The price system is unusual. The prices for perfumes and cosmetics come from a book and are quoted to you as duty-free prices, minus a 20% discount. All other merchandise—the store is filled with French luxury goods of all sorts—has price tags that are at full retail, so you must deduct 20% in order to get an accurate price. As a rule of thumb, Roger Albert is $1 less expensive than the established Caribbean price for the same merchandise in china and crystal; the perfumes, like perfumes everywhere, vary by brand but are fixed throughout the Caribbean like everyone else's.

However, the store is large and clean and trimmed with blue lapis lazuli borders, and is without question the best place in town to shop. I have been here at 9:15am, and it is devoid of tourists, even with a ship in port. Sometimes there are crowds, so I like to get here early. There is a watch store portion of Roger Albert next door and a small cigar shop with humidor in the rear.

You get lots of little samples when you buy perfume; show this book and get a complete gift bag of samples.

PHARMACIES

ALAIN BUCHER
Corner of rue de la République and rue Blénac.

Although this is not the best pharmacy in town, it was the first I discovered as I prowled the back streets of Fort-de-France, and I almost burst into tears—all those French beauty products are like old friends to me. This is conveniently located and stocked with basics like Orangine and Vichy.

 **PHARMACIE SAINT ROSE**
67 rue Lamartine.

Bigger, better, more equipped with some of the French diet pills and slimming gimmicks.

ET VENDORS

LE VERGER ANTILLAIS.
Blvd. Alfassa, Fort-de-France.

Bien sur, 5F for the mango and thanks for the memories. Mangoes are less in Barbados but more at my hometown Stop & Shop.

Fort-de-France on a Schedule: The Vive La France Tour

1. Fort-de-France is a real town. It is not cute, it is not quaint, it is not touristy . . . well, almost not. Finding your way around is easy. Make your first stop the Tourist Information Center on the waterfront at Boulevard Alfassa. Pick up a map here, and then stop in next door at the Caribbean Art Center. The exhibits change regularly, and you just might be there at the right time to pick up a handmade gift or a wonderful piece of art.

2. Across the street in La Savane Park is the flea market, which is the other source of tourist items in town. The stalls are set up early in the morning and have a full selection of tourist fans, straw hats, conch shells, and dolls.

3. Directly across the street, you will see the signs for **Roger Albert.** His large duty-free shop is located on Avenue Victor Hugo, with another smaller entrance on rue Ernest Deproge. Stop in here and take a quick tour around the perfume, Lalique, and Baccarat counters. You will probably do most of your shopping here, so you might as well know what he sells. If you can't find a better deal elsewhere in town, you will know what to look forward to. If you have a very limited time in town we recommend that you come here and stay here. The prices are competitive with all of the other islands, and the atmosphere is friendly and professional. Remember, there are only about six duty-free shops in town anyway.

4. Walk out of the main entrance onto Avenue Victor Hugo and take a left. This is one of the main shopping streets in town. Tour in and out of the resort boutiques until you reach rue Schoelcher, where you will take a right. Stop in at **Au Printemps** (No. 12) and check out the perfume counter. It helps to speak French here.

5. Continue along rue Schoelcher until you reach rue Perrinon, where you will want to take a left. Stop in at the boutiques along the way until you reach the flea market at the corner of rue Isambert. The flea market is not upscale, but it does offer some interesting things from time to time. Take a left and another left onto rue Saint-Louis three blocks down. The name of the street at this point is rue Saint-Louis, but it will turn into rue Antoine Siger. This is the real people section of Fort-de-France.

6. Walk back along rue Antoine Siger, stopping in at **Charles Jourdan** and **Sinamon,** for shoes. As

you get closer to rue de la Liberté the shops get nicer.

7. Now you are ready to go back to **Roger Albert** and finish your shopping. It's even better here the second time around.

ST. MARTIN / ST. MAARTEN

. . . .

Excusez moi, I have named this chapter French Caribbean and included a small part of Holland. *Mon Dieu!*

So let's just say welcome and double welcome to an island with two personalities, two nationalities (French and Dutch), and two shopping cities (Marigot and Philipsburg). I haven't got a chapter called Dutch Caribbean (sorry about that), so you are just going to have to cope. *Bonne chance.*

Now then, to get on with it, both of the main cities of the island (quick, sing a chorus: I've looked at both sides now . . .) were devastated by Hurricane Luis several years ago but are just now recovering. While most of the buildings have been rebuilt, I haven't found that the islands feel the same, deep down. I think a lot of retailers were frustrated and simply quit; I think a lot of the retail shops are owned by a whole new set of people.

Maybe in a few years and after the new $30-million pier facility and Courthouse Promenade are in place, maybe the community will pull together and sparkle anew. You'll just have to keep coming back year after to year to see how it's going.

While the two sides of the island have always felt very different from each other, I've never felt such a chasm between them as on my last visit. Philipsburg does get most of the cruise traffic, but I think smart shoppers may enjoy a little trip to the French side of the island. (Hence the organization of this chapter with emphasis on the French.)

Even a day visit allows you plenty of time to shop both sides, so don't panic. I have divided this chapter into the two parts that are most commonly visited, for easier use. I've eliminated discussion of Grand Case because its changed a lot and you don't go there to shop, especially if you are in town for a day via cruise ship.

Island Cities

PHILIPSBURG

Philipsburg is the Dutch capital city and the main port of St. Maarten. If you were hoping for shopping cutes the likes of Curaçao, which also has Dutch roots, no such luck. There are two rather nice nouveau-Dutch developments: brand-new buildings that have scalloped facades and are painted in rainbow colors and trimmed with white gingerbread. But mostly, Philipsburg is not cute.

On the other hand, Philipsburg does have some buys. Most duty-free items are better priced in Philipsburg, and yes, Philipsburg prices can be less than prices on the French side for same or similar merchandise. Branches of the same store keep their prices standard, however. Please note that for the most part, there isn't too much cross-over with stores or with merchandise on the two sides or in the two main towns.

Even the Little Switzerland in Philipsburg is vastly different from the Little Switzerland in Marigot. Read on.

MARIGOT

Capital city of the French side of the island, Marigot sprawls around and offers stores in all sorts of places. It's not very cute, either, but it has some charm, and it's certainly more with-it and service-oriented than Philipsburg. Can you imagine, the French side is actually friendly?

Marigot is a walk-and-see-and-explore-down-the-side-street kind of place, very different from Philipsburg's one-main-drag system. While there is some French colonial feeling to the city, this is not New Orleans, no matter what anyone tells you.

Getting Around the Island

Getting around the whole island is something worth doing because there are lots of cities and resorts to poke into and soak up. If you really love to shop, you'll want to leave the beach and the punch drinks long enough to do it up proud and get to both halves of the whole scene.

Very few cruise ships dock in Marigot, so you will probably arrive in Marigot by taxi, which should cost about $10 U.S. from Philipsburg. You can make a deal with your driver to come back at a certain time; your resort can always call you a cab if you aren't with a cruise ship. Or you can flag a taxi at the waterfront at Marigot's main taxi stand right on the rue de France—there's a main queue right in the heart of the harborfront area, which has been restored and redeveloped and snazzed up.

If you arrive on the island by plane, taxis at the airport work on a flat-rate system. Some resorts send a van or a car for you.

While shopping around town, either town, you can easily walk and wander. But you might want to look at a map, since the shops are not laid out in a row in Marigot.

Philipsburg is far more crowded than Marigot and much harder to drive through; expect a traffic jam on the main street (Front Street), and avoid driving around major cities in rush hours, as traffic can be tight. My last taxi driver insisted on driving completely around the island the long way in order to avoid traffic on the direct road between Marigot and Philipsburg.

Expect to pay between $10 to $15 U.S. for a one-way ride between the two main cities on the island; $15 is the cost of the long way around. Taxis are plentiful, but drivers may be rude—and I don't mean French drivers, believe me. If you are doing the long way, you will automatically drive through Grand Case, so get the driver to slow down and show you what's there.

Money Matters

Prices on the French side of the island are listed in francs, or in francs and dollars. Most shops take any of three or four different currencies, as well as plastic. Beware the rate of exchange on the franc, as the bargains come and go with the strength of the dollar. As we go to press, the dollar is feeling a little stronger than usual against the franc, and it makes shopping in the French Caribbean all that more jolly, or *jolie*.

Because this is the same franc that is used in France (duh), you can use any spare change you have left over from a trip to Europe. Or you can jump ship, stay 'til you are bored, and then fly on Air France directly to Paris to spend the rest of your money. It's just a thought . . .

Philipsburg prices are not related to the franc, nor do they seem to have a lot to do with florins, even though that is the official currency. Prices are most often listed in U.S. dollars.

Taxi drivers have readily taken dollars from me on both sides of the island.

My Island for a Mall

Marina Port La Royale (Marigot)   Built to accommodate the many boats that pull into the sheltered harbor to the north of Marigot, Port La Royale has grown and grown and is still growing. The newest development is a two-story addition to the side. Look for a complete selection of resort clothing in all price ranges. Styles range from yuppie to teen chic; there's even a **Maxim's** for the foodies.

Poke your nose into: **Sonia Rykiel, Naf Naf, Le Bastrinque, Lipstick, Jennifer & Company,** and **Desmo,** the Italian handbag firm, among others. It's really a very pleasant fairyland over here—boats, water, a little sprawl that makes you think there's something to explore and some shops where window shopping is perfectly okay.

Amsterdam Shopping Center (Round Pond)   On the outskirts of Philipsburg, if you are coming or going on the back road to the north of the island (this is the opposite side from Juliana Mullet), you will pass another cutie-pie shopping center in the Dutch architectural style I like so much. This one is really for locals more than tourists, but it's fun to look at anyway.

Shopping Hours

On the Dutch side, stores are open nonstop 9am to 6pm, Monday through Saturday. On the French side, most stores close for *midi* (midday lunch break) at 12:30pm and reopen at 2 or 2:30pm. They are open until 7pm or later.

SUNDAY SHOPPING

When there's a cruise ship in town on a Sunday (which is frequently; a schedule of arriving ships is always posted on the front page of *St. Maarten This Month* in a column called "Cruise Calls"), about half of the stores in Philipsburg are open.

Marigot is pretty dead on Sundays, but some shops do open for ships. *Dimanche* has never been a big day in retail for the French.

Landlubber's Delight

LA SAMANNA
Long Bay (Baie Longue). ☎ *800/854-2252 in the U.S., or 590/87-64-00.*

This is the fanciest resort in town, a dream come true for those who can afford to stay here. We are talking $500 a night in season.

I like to come here for lunch as part of my cruise day. You sit on the terrace; eat divine food; soak up French Provençale fabrics and style; look at the flowers, the bushes, and the sand and sea, and oh yes, the rich people who surround you. It's worth 50 bucks just to be part of it. Closed September to October.

FRENCH SIDE: ST. MARTIN

Bienvenue à Marigot

From the water, the town of Marigot looks small and sleepy. But yawn no more, *cherie*. The main shopping seems to be concentrated on rue de la République and rue de la Liberté; but wait, there is another whole section of shopping off to the side, down rue du Général de Gaulle, that leads to the Marina Port La Royale Center. The harborfront has been totally redeveloped (this is a good news/bad news kind of thing), so that it remains not only the heart of the port and the town, but a clean and spiffy tourist center. It's a little too new for me, a little too calculated (bring in da funk), but you can't ignore that it's nice.

Fashions are from France and Italy, with some English china and crystal thrown in. I think the prices are as good as you will find. The only problem with going crazy here is that you will get a better U.S. Customs allowance from St. Thomas. Also, the strength of the dollar will affect the strength of your bargain.

Many people like the idea that Marigot wanders—the stores are here and there and everywhere, not in a straight row as in Philipsburg and most other island cities. While there is a nest of stores right where you expect to find them, up against the water and at the flagpole, there are more stores on the side streets, the back streets, and in an ever-increasing number of malls and strips.

Many of the stores look small and not so charming, yet plastered to the windows are the logos of the designers we all love to love. All shops bear investigating because first glances can't give you a firm decision on if the shopping here is really what you were expecting. This isn't Cannes, or even Martinique, but you can get some good buys and fill in your French needs.

Also note that if you want to call the U.S., use your trusty France Telecom card at the pay phones at the waterfront or buy a France Telecom card and use it to call the U.S. (or France). Since France Telecom is the local provider, you get the best rates this way.

There is a fruit, veggie, and craft market at the harborfront in Marigot; some days its fun and funky but mostly it's sort of down and out and cheap and hippie dippie. *C'est la vie.*

Finds

MANEKS
Rue de la République.

The local TT (tourist trap) and a funny funky one at that, this is the stop for T-shirts, hats, sun lotion, postcards, and more. Shirts run from $6 to $17; my favorite take-home gifts are shell and piranha magnets for the refrigerator and little plastic bags of sand from local beaches. T-shirt designs in Marigot are disappointing, although Maneks seems to have the best selection in town.

This is a solid source for postcards because they sell cards that are reproductions of the works of local artists. The local postcards are especially charming; you'll see them also at the Shipwreck Shop in Philipsburg as well. These cards are usually market scenes or island scenes done in vivid colors and finally giving a taste of the vision of Caribbean style. It's a far better card to send to friends than one more perfect beach shot. You may have to go a whopping

5F (about $1) per card, but if you care about image, you will appreciate these artworks.

I bought a few cigars here, although there are a ton of cigar shops over at Marina Port La Royale, and there's also a very good cigar shop on the other side.

LITTLE SWITZERLAND
Rue de la Liberté, Marigot.

Okay, this is tricky. Yes *(mais oui)*, there is also a Little Switzerland shop on the Dutch side, but no, *(non, non, non)* they are not very similar and *non,* they don't have the same stuff!

Little Switzerland is one of the most famous stores in the Caribbean for duty-free luxury items, and you'll do yourself, and this store, a disservice by shopping only in the Philipsburg store.

Prices on those items carried in both stores are identical on both sides of the island, as well as in other Caribbean ports. The perfume selection doesn't seem as large once you've seen a really good selection, but the basics are here, and if you happen on a sale or close-outs, you can do well.

The deal is: *Un,* it's one of the few **Hermès** duty-free shops in the Caribe, and *deux,* you get a great selection of big-name French leather goods such as **Didier Lamarthe** and **Ines de la Fressange** that they have never even heard of on the Dutch side. Also, the subtext of what this shop feels like is quite unique; it feels fancy. There's light and air and space and elegance; most Caribbean stores, even nice ones, are crammed with stuff and you have no feeling of finesse. Here, there is luxury in the air. If you aren't going on to St. Barts, you won't find much luxury like this anywhere else.

ORO DE SOL
Rue de la République and blvd. de France (harborfront), Marigot.

One of those general stores, like Little Switzerland, that sells a little of everything: china, crystal, perfume, watches, and more. There are two different stores that house the whole thing, a half block apart.

Very nice stuff, representing many of the world's big names in deluxe goods; even designer linens are sold here. (This is a first for the Caribbean, outside of Bermuda.) I'll take the Lalique jewelry, thank you and *merci bien.*

LIPSTICK
Rue de la République, Marigot.

There's another branch of Lipstick on the Dutch side, so you can buy there. This store is small but packed with French beauty products and perfumes. There's another branch in Marina Port La Royale. Lipstick carries Guerlain makeup. I sometimes buy discontinued colors at cut-rate prices here; look in the little baskets on the counters or for the *soldes* signs.

MIDTOWN MUSIC
Rue de la République.

Get your Johnny Hallyday here. It's not cheap, but when you're in love with the sound of Johnny, what can you do.

PASSIONS
Marina Port La Royale

Where would women be without their dreams of French jewelry? I'm the one who is dreaming that someday I will get the Van Der Bauwede leather bracelet with gold all over it. If you have no idea what I am talking about, read French *Vogue* or do a little window shopping over here. Poiray is also sold here. Oh, la la.

LA CASA DEL HABANO
Marina Port La Royale.

Just like the name says, another cigar joint. This one far fancier than Maneks, but it is over at the port's mall on the other side of town. The very best Cuban brands. This is a branch of a chain; there are two other cigar shops in the marina as well.

DUTCH SIDE: ST. MAARTEN

. . . .

Going Dutch

Not that you'll see too many tulips, or boys and girls in their Hans Brinker suits with hand-painted wooden clogs, but the shopping on the Dutch side of this small island is intense, and the **Delft Blue Gallery** does sell the Delft ceramics you are dreaming of. Beyond that, the Dutch side really represents much more standard Caribbean fare: tons of jewelry stores, several big general stores that sell everything, a large and gorgeous **Ralph Lauren/Polo** shop, which is not a factory store. Oh yes, there's a whole lot of shopping going down in Philipsburg.

Often there are so many cruise passengers in the streets that traffic cannot get by. You might want to head to Marigot in the morning and let the crowds thin out here and return after lunch.

The stores in Philipsburg are not very glamorous from the street, and that's a fact. There are a few exceptions here—**Old Street, Ralph Lauren, Lipstick**—but if you have fantasies of cutes, drop them now. While the city is by no means postcard perfect, there are several examples of Caribbean style in terms of architecture or paint that are visually enticing; don't miss a hard stare at the **West Indian Tavern** (even if you don't eat here, stare at it), which is hand-painted in hot colors and trimmed with white gingerbread. Even the lampposts are orange.

At the other end of Front Street from the West Indian Tavern is **L'Escargot,** another piece of delicious architecture, design, and paint colors. Also walk into a lot of the stores just to see them; many hold hidden surprises that are fun to look at. You don't have to buy.

It also is great fun to be walking along the street thinking of bargains and to suddenly come to a space between stores where you can peer through and see a patch of blue, blue water, and maybe even some sand. Sailboats float on the horizon, and you are certain you have found the best of all possible worlds.

Don't forget that on this side of the island, the name of the place is often spelled Sint Maarten, which is the Dutch influence. There's more Dutch influence in the names of a few of the stores, which are branches of retailers in the old country, or in the use of the word "Amsterdam." The architecture can be highly Dutch, as in the nouveau-colonial style of Old Street, Maho Reef, and Amsterdam Shopping Centers, or quasi-Dutch, such as the stores that are painted bright turquoise inside.

Philipsburg Resources

Booze

If you are just visiting St. Maarten (that is, you're not on a cruise that goes to St. Thomas), you will want to buy liquor on the Dutch side of the island rather than the French, although prices are the same. St. Maarten has relatively good prices on liquor, but the U.S. Customs allowance is so much better from the U.S. Virgin Islands (and who wants to schelp around a bottle or two?) that you should wait if you can. Otherwise, stop in any of the general stores in Philipsburg, try out the **Rams Warehouse** in Salt Pond if you're feeling wild and crazy, or just buy at **Rams** on Front Street. Remember, you are only allowed to bring in one liter from a non U.S.V.I. destination.

Many shops will ask you to sample the local specialty liquer, made with guavaberries.

CAMERAS & ELECTRONICS

RAMS
Front St.

The leading store in town for electronic equipment and bargaining. The store is run by some very clever businesspeople who have done their research and, whenever possible, sell their product for just slightly less than St. Thomas.

CARIBBEAN STYLE

SHIPWRECK SHOP
Front St.

The best store on the island for arts and crafts that don't look like straw-market tourist finds. Stock up on postcards (the artsy kind), batiks, hand-painted boxes, and all sorts of gift items and doodads. Much of it comes from the West Indies but a good bit of it seems to come from the Merchandise Mart in Miami. Who cares?

Since the hurricane, the new version of the store lacks the same charm the old one had, and it is becoming more and more like a fancy TT and mini-mart, but that's no reason not to shop here.

DESIGNERS

The leading designer shop of the area is the stunning **Ralph Lauren/Polo** shop which they tell me is a franchise. It is not to be confused with the Ralph Lauren owned factory stores in the Caribbean (one in San Juan, one in St. Croix) nor with Mexican Ralph Lauren/Polo which is made in Mexico (legally). Besides Ralph, there's **Tommy Hilfiger** (Old Street) and **Lacoste** (Front Street). Lacoste was very, very expensive.

I cannot swear to you about the authenticity of these goods or their value; the Ralph Lauren costs more than at the outlets but less than in the U.S. at regular retail. I'm certain the Lacoste is real but I don't know if it is U.S. Lacoste or French Lacoste; French does cost more.

GENERAL STORES

LITTLE SWITZERLAND
Front St.

Large double store that sells everything; see listing below for jewelry. There's also everything else.

NEW AMSTERDAM STORE
Front St.

One of those general stores that sells everything, this is a very deep store that seems to keep on going. There's an upstairs also. The store seems to sell a little of everything in selling circles or groups of counters—all the big names from Polo to Swatch to Le Clip, and more. Many designer and big-manufacturer names are here; prices are fixed to the same as other shops on the island. They do a big business in linens, of the Hong Kong type. Very competitive and complete; open Sunday.

ASHBURY'S
Front St.

I have very mixed emotions as I write about this store because it confuses me and I don't know how to best express myself without going to jail. The store has a lot of stuff and I shop here and I love to look at everything and I have bought some super things, such as a pair of Christain Lacroix sunglasses marked down from $180 to $20. My problem is that I cannot swear that all the designer stuff comes from France.

Ashbury's has this very chic brochure with color pictures from the designers and a list of the addresses of their five stores dotted all over the Basin (there is also one in Marigot). On the back of this brochure is a coupon for 10% off your purchases in luggage, jewelry, crystal, sunglasses, or leather goods. They carry more categories of goods than this, but you can use the discount coupon in these areas.

JEWELRY

LITTLE SWITZERLAND
Front St.

Now this is a store. The one in Marigot is totally different; let the smart shopper do them both!

This branch, one of the best of the many Little Switzerlands all over the Caribbean, is a joy to shop for the big names of china, crystal, perfume, and more. They have a little, sometimes a lot, of everything. Prices are the same as at other stores like this, so you're shopping for selection, style, and stock. But with general stores such as this and Oro de Sol, you can buy it all, go broke, and head for the beach in no time at all.

TREASURE COVE
Front St.

One of several very nice jewelry stores where you'll go nuts over chains, charms, and gold. Treasure Cove is pink with white trim and sports a striped awning; it looks a lot like Little Switzerland, and you may get mixed up as to where you are.

Even more confusing is the fact that there is a branch of Little Switzerland next door, but it has wood shingles in an attempt to de-confuse you.

H. STERN JEWELERS
Front St.

I am friends with Hans Stern, but I also think he's the best jeweler in the Caribbean. The store is brand new post-Luis and one of the nicest stores in town. No reason to wait for St. Thomas.

LIL EUROPE
Front St.

One of many jewelry shops competing for business along Front Street, Lil Europe impressed me with good prices on items I had previously priced in Hong Kong. In most cases, Lil Europe was cheaper on the Italian-made items. Specifically, the 18-carat gold-link necklace that years ago I had seen in Hong Kong for $1,000 was $860 here. Much of the merchandise is not top quality, but if you have a good eye, this is an important find.

MALLS

OLD STREET
Off Front St.

Hats off to the developer who came up with this gem. We appreciate real-estate developers who know how to do things our way; so whoever you are, kisses to you and yours. Old Street is a long passageway between buildings on the far end of Front Street and is a rather new development that is very Dutch, with much colored stucco and gingerbread. The buildings are painted bright Caribbean Dutch colors; the tiles are all hand-painted in blue and white. Bistros have outdoor seating areas, and there is even a gazebo bar at the far end, painted bright sun yellow. The shops are good tourist fare, including a Ralph Lauren/Polo shop—or should we say, a shop that sells Ralph Lauren and has giant Polo painted windows. It's small, but nice, and sells the basics at about 15% less than U.S. retail prices. The factory outlet in San Juan has better prices; there is another store in Marigot that also sells Lauren at similar prices to the factory outlet store. Both St. Maarten stores sell first quality.

Perfume

Lipstick
Front St.

Spacious modern store, next door to Ralph Lauren and across the street from Old Street—yep, this is the best part of town. They have a shop on the French side that I like to visit.

The One Day in Town/Both Sides Now Tour

Pop right into a taxi first thing in the morning, and head for the French side, St. Martin. St. Martin has many little villages and one main town, Marigot. They will close for lunch, so the plan is to get there early and beat the other tourists and enjoy the stores and the shopping opportunities.

The shops are scattered around town; the streets seem to make no sense, but that is only because of the zigzag way they have been laid out. Who cares? *Vive la France!*

Start at the main turnaround, called **Market Square.** The tourist bureau has a stand across the street. You will be on Boulevard de France. Stop in at the shops here before heading up rue de la République. This is the main street and has the best serious shopping, even though it certainly is not what it was before Hurricane Luis!

Now take rue Maurasse, which will eventually lead you to rue du Général de Gaulle. Walk through the shopping development and poke into **Milano Magia, Jet Set, Patrick Sport,** and **Benetton.**

You will now be at the junction of rue de Président Kennedy and the entrance to the **Port La Royale** shopping complex. This is a fun place to stop for lunch or "un Coca" and admire the pretty boats in the harbor.

The shopping is casual resort wear, drop-dead chic French diamonds and jewelry, cigars, and rich dudes with their yachts and blonde wives.

On your way back to town, walk down rue d'Anguille, which runs into rue de la Liberté. These streets parallel rue du Général de Gaulle, but are closer to the water. Stop for a crêpe, have a cafe au lait, listen to the sound of France. Or just pop into any harborfront bistro for lunch.

Return to Philipsburg after lunch.

Once back in Philipsburg, head to the heart of town at the pier, although a new pier facility is expected in the not-too-distant future.

Along the pier are a number of blankets set up selling straw goods and handmade craft items. Remember what you see in case you want to buy something before returning to the ship.

If you are facing the sea, take a right on the main street, Front Street. This isn't the better end of town, so you have the better part of town to look forward to when you finish seeing the stores at this end and head for Old Street and Polo/Ralph Lauren, which are in the best parts of town. There's also several jewelry shops and **Little Switzerland** on the "good" end of Front Street.

Don't spend all your earnings at **H. Stern** because you want to save some for good old Old Street. This is one of my favorite developments in all of the islands. The architecture is a replica of the original Dutch buildings that probably were never this cute in the first place.

The stores are the better quality variety, including a **Tommy Hilfiger** shop. The farther end of Front Street after Old Street is mostly restaurants and hotels.

ST. BARTS

This is all in the telling, except the telling is not in the pronounciation but in the writing. *Regardez*, if you are really "in" or you are French, you write "St. Barths," which is pronounced the same as St. Barts, but it has to do with French grammatical rules and the fact that you are using the nickname for an island called St. Barthélémy, after Christopher Columbus' brother. As pretentious as I love to be, I am still going to use the St. Barts form in this portion of the book, but note that other guidebooks and French language signs will use the other spelling.

St. Barts is one of the most unusual Caribbean islands in that it's fancier and chicer than most, it's very hard to reach, and the locals don't want cruiseship business. Only a few ships are even small enough to put in at St. Barts, and therein lies its cachet and the *charme*.

Christie Brinkley met Billy Joel on St. Barts, Mick (Jagger, not Mouse) hangs on St. Barts, Princess Di was a regular before she discovered Barbuda and the K Club. If you understand the very basic rule of the jet set, that the good places are hard to get to, you grasp the whole scene. All of the most exclusive resorts in the world are hard to get to; this eliminates the hoi-polloi. At St. Barts, the island is so exclusive that locals really don't want to ruin the place and they certainly don't want tourist business or giant luxury liners overflowing with Americans waving credit cards.

The Lay of the Land

Gustavia is the capital city and the port where ships (and yachts, *bien sur*) come to visit; it is on the southern- and western-most portion of an almost V-shaped island. Directly across from Gustavia on the other shore of the island is the Bay St. Jean. Although there is also a town called Marigot on this island, do not confuse it with Marigot on St. Martin.

Landlubber's Delight

I found more chic hotels here than on any other island; I list just three below, because I think you're visiting for the day and possibly looking to inspect a hotel, have some lunch, see and be seen, and not stay for a week. If you are actually looking for a longer stay, also check out **Le Toiny, The Taiwana,** and **Hotel St. Barth Isle de France.** If you're slumming it and can only budget about $250 per night, seek out **Filao Beach Hotel.**

HÔTEL GUANAHANI
Grand Cul-de-Sac. ☎ *800/932-3222 in the U.S., or 590/27-66-60.*

Knowing how to pronounce the name of the hotel *(Gwan-a-hanee)* is the key; my in to the inn is that I met the man who is the General Manager (Marc Thésé) in Nice when he sat next to me at a dinner party and charmed me to death. Add to that the genius of Grace Leo, who designs and collects hotels of enormous importance (The Lancaster in Paris, The Clarence in Dublin) and obviously, you have a place to visit before you die. This is not actually the fanciest hotel in town, but I like to think of it as my place. There are two beaches, and yes, you can come to eat—seek **L'Indigo** at the pool, although there is also a fancy restaurant on hand.

CARL GUSTAF RESORT
Rue des Normands, Gustavia. ☎ *800/322-2223 in the U.S., or 590/27-82-83; fax 590/27-82-37*

This is very private and "in" and celebrity oriented; you might not be comfortable if you aren't a personal friend of photographer Patrick Demarchelier.

EDEN ROCK
St.-Jean Bay. ☎ *590/27-72-94.*

It has reopened, it has expanded, it has arrived— Eden Rock now has nine bedrooms for guests and a sensational place to eat lunch.

Snack & Shop

La Select
Gustavia

The most famous cheeseburger in the Caribbean.

Maya's
Public. ☎ *590/27-75-73.*

For 10 years, the most "in" place in town. Bar scene, too.

The Shopping Scene

Shopping is done either in downtown Gustavia or in the local *hypermarché* where one pigs out on French imports. Never mind the price, darling; if you have to ask . . .

Storekeepers try to guard the privacy of the clientele, are anti-real people, and don't want to know from cruise passengers. Many shops actually close up if a ship is in town; there was what's now called the Boutique Revolution during which store owners closed up in order to discourage ships from even including the island on their itineraries.

It's so hard to be carelessly chic. **Hermès** does a huge business, of course (they sell a lot of beach towels!), and **Gucci** is very cute with its ochre plantation-style Caribbean wooden building with dark green shutters. Also check out **Free Mousse,** for lotions and potions.

A trip to the Gustavia market is a must do, especially to load up on aromatic oils and the local bug spray of the moment made by Helene and Franck Garcia whose label is Belou P.

Chapter Eleven

· · · · · · · ·

THE SOUTHERN CARIBBEAN: BARBADOS & ANTIGUA

WELCOME TO BARBADOS

· ·

Barbados. The very sound of it rustles in the breeze, conjures up mental images of beautiful black ladies in billowing skirts, tiered with ruffles and crinolines and bright as a Caribbean patchwork. Ladies with baskets on their heads, bracelets on their arms, and smiles in their eyes. Pirates. Stately mansions. Sugarcane. Rum.

Shopping?

Hmmm, well, yes and no.

You see, Barbados is one of my favorite islands, and I think if I were forced (by pirates, of course) to spend a week on any one island, I would pick a week at Sandy Lane. But not for the shopping. I'd only venture out every now and then and possibly never even go into downtown Bridgetown.

Arriving in Barbados

The docking facilities at the port on the outskirts of Georgetown are enormous, so you may actually be bused from your ship to the terminal, depending on which berth your cruise liner occupies. If you've never been here before, you may get the sense that you are in the middle of nowhere. Not to worry.

The cruise terminal, officially named Deepwater Cruise Pier, is relatively new and is sensational. You can actually do all your island shopping here, or shop first, then tour, and then finish up your day before you get on the ship with more shopping. All of the best stores in downtown have a branch in the terminal.

Better yet, the terminal actually has two parts: the terminal mall itself and then an additional chattel house–style mall to the rear, filled with stalls selling crafts and tourist items, with a cafe, with women willing to braid your hair or create a set of dreads, and more. There are phones here; there's also an entire calling station (I called England for all of $4, rather impressive considering how outrageous international long distance can be). You can buy film, booze, suntan oil, and visit the Tourist Office, all right at the terminal building.

Oh yes, you can also arrive by plane. The Concorde flies in from Britain regularly in season and on some charters from the U.S.

Money Matters

Local currency is pegged at half the value of the U.S. dollar so $2 Barbadian equal $1 U.S.

Barbados Neighborhoods

Barbados is divided into several parishes. The two most famous areas (aside from Bridgetown) are on the southeast coast—where Sam Lord's is—and the west coast (on the Caribbean side) around Speightstown and Holetown, directly north of Bridgetown and home of the big-time resorts.

The rocky east coast (which borders the Atlantic Ocean) is beautiful to look at, nice to drive around, but has many portions that are too dangerous for swimming. Our favorite town happens to be Oistins, a fishing village we think is loaded with charm, although lacking in a Valentino boutique.

If you are in Bridgetown for a day, try to make a deal with a taxi driver at the port to drive you all around. If you're here for more than a day, rent a car (or a "moke," a golf-cartlike jeep) and plan to get lost. The roads aren't too well marked, and residents do drive on the "wrong side of the road," but you certainly can't drive to China, so get lost and have fun. There is a lot to look at and enjoy. Should you just want to enjoy the beaches, don't feel guilty—the beaches are stunning and often filled with vendors! You might decide that you want to do a chattel-house look around. The island is dotted with old chattel houses that are pretty much falling apart and new chattel houses that have become the latest vogue in retail architecture. They are fun and stunning and give you a very bright welcome. While other nearby islands also use this type of architecture, the best examples are found in Barbados.

BRIDGETOWN

If this is your first trip to Barbados and you think you are going to see the wonders of a great island by heading downtown, think again. There's terrific shopping right at the cruise pier. You can spend a little bit of time downtown; but please, don't make a day of it, and please, get out and find out what this island really feels like, and don't judge it by downtown.

There isn't a lot of shopping in Bridgetown. In fact, you can get the best of Bridgetown in an $1^{1}/_{2}$ hours and be gone. Off toward Mount Gay and Sandy Lane.

Thoughts about town:

- Expect nothing, so if you like it here, you can be pleasantly surprised.
- Don't believe anything you read in any guidebook, brochure, or cruise sheet. Remain skeptical so your fantasies can't be dashed and you don't get depressed.

- Keep reminding yourself that the shopping at the pier is actually excellent and that the ship is stopping in St. Thomas anyway. If perchance you are not going on to St. Thomas, you are still going somewhere that probably has better shopping than Bridgetown.

It's not that the shopping is so bad in Bridgetown; it's that the stores are *sooo* lacking in charm.

On many cruises, Barbados is the first port because it is the farthest away. This is good because it's an excellent chance to do homework without getting swept away. Have your homework sheets or notepad ready in your purse, so you can compare prices from home to those in some of the duty frees. Only pounce on items that are on sale in reputable shops.

If you see it in Barbados and love it, there is no reason NOT to buy it. You will not find the item cheaper in another port—the prices will be the same. (This applies to china and crystal, not cameras and electronics.)

Ask about stock on a certain item if you are serious about it but want to think on it. If you come in with a cruise ship, and the store only has three of this vase you love, and you see it in the morning and expect it will still be there in the afternoon, think twice. Don't make any assumptions. My experience is that stores in Barbados do not have a lot of stock, especially in the summer.

Don't think that rum is rum and you can get it anywhere. You can get some brands of rum anywhere, but other islands do not necessarily have a good selection of your island's best buys. If you want to try the fabled Mount Gay rum, buy it in Barbados.

The Lay of the Land

The main drag is Broad Street—it leads from Trafalgar Square to where the ships dock. (Which is in the middle of nowhere.) The whole city is easily walkable. (Although you can walk the 2 miles from ship to town, it is a pretty boring walk and the sun can be very hot.)

Most of Bridgetown is for the locals. There are some shops along Broad Street set up for the bargain-hunting tourists, but you will be hard put to find an attractive facade or too many inviting shops to drool over. They have all of the usual crystal and china, but brother, these guys don't know from ambience.

All is not lost. If you get out of Bridgetown and drive around, you will be impressed by the teeny villages, the every-here-and-a-while good boutiques, the adorable houses painted in razzmatazz-then-rainwashed colors, and the charm of the place. I've taken photographs that could go in a book on Caribbean style. There are isolated places of beauty; there is architecture and charm to enjoy—out of Bridgetown.

Landlubber's Delight

HILTON INTERNATIONAL BARBADOS
Needham's Point, St. Michael.
☎ *800/HILTONS or 809/426-0200.*

I happen to be a big Hilton fan in the Caribbean and am proud to say I've been visiting this particular Hilton for over 10 years. The hotel is right outside of Bridgetown (you could walk the 2 miles) and seems to be built into an old fort or something. The hotel is toward the island's Atlantic side, away from the glittery west coast where the swankiest hotels are located; this is a hotel for real people, not movie stars.

It has a three-deck lobby with a jungle inside it and a gorgeous private beach. Best yet, this Hilton has a shopping arcade, probably the best one in the area. While the stores are small and there are only about seven of them, you do not need to go to town. Everything you want is sold nicely here, so enjoy.

There's a branch of **Harrison's,** there's a store for liquor, and there are a few T-shirt shops.

Some cruise ships have tie-ins for day-trippers. If you're here for several days, the package deals are great; the flying fish served alfresco on the beach are memorable.

SANDY LANE
St. James. ☎ 800/225-5843 in the U.S. and Canada, or 809/432-1311.

When I die and go to heaven, I will land at Sandy Lane. Before that, I am content with getting off a ship, taking a taxi to Speightstown and St. James and then ending up at Sandy Lane for lunch and luxury. Even if you just come for an iced coffee at an off-hour and sit outside under a parasol to stare at everyone and everything, you owe it to yourself to experience this version of the Caribbean. This, friends, is what it's all about.

The hotel is a member of Leading Hotels Great Affordables Program, with a five-night stay for those who aren't on a cruise or want to pick up a cruise in town. There are also other plans depending on the season and whether or not you want meals at the hotel included and what sort of view you want. On the Affordable Program, April 15 to November 15, you get a ton of inclusives plus breakfast and dinner for about $450 a night, which happens to be a bargain for this sort of thing. This is for two people, not per person.

Snack & Shop

WATERFRONT CAFÉ
Harborfront, Bridgetown.

Everyone seems to end up at the Waterfront Café, a pub sort of place where you can eat a burger or simply cool down with a lime squash. They also serve flying fish sandwiches.

RANDY'S TAXI SERVICE
☎ *246/437-4871*

Randy made our day-trip to Barbados wonderful; call him and book ahead—he'll work out a day price (about $75 to $100) or a half-day price with you, meet you at the cruise terminal, wait for you wherever you want to wander, and he won't even drink while at the Mount Gay Rum factory. He'll also work out special rates for repeat customers. The car phone number is 230-5890.

SHOPS OF THE GINGERBREAD HOUSE
Hincks St., Bridgetown.

If you explore the other part of downtown away from the harborfront, you'll end up on this street which is still trying to develop into a shopping area. The Shops of the Gingerbread House form a mini-mall where you can get an iced cappuccino.

Local Designs & Crafts

Although each of the Caribbean Islands has a few local designers or folk artists who make it at least regionally if not globally, Barbados has a highly developed design scene in ready-to-wear and beach clothing. The designs are usually very tropical and not the kind of stuff you would wear once out of the Caribbean, although some of it might do in Polynesia. Bold slashes of color or of flowers painted across cotton are offered up by many designers in the boutiques along the waterfront in Bridgetown and at hotel boutiques.

Among the most famous of local clothing designers is **Carol Cadogan,** who has her own shop on the far side of downtown, on the way to the Hilton; her line is called Cotton Days, but it is much more dressy and Viva Las Vegas than tropical or resorty. I went wild for a dress by local artist Angela B that was very resorty and tropical and also several hundred dollars and way out of my league—but it was fabulous. **Sandbox,** designed by two local women, has been featured on the BBC Clothes Show in the U.K.

If you're more interested in pottery, head for **Chalky Mount** where there's a studio and a store; you need a car to get there. Once on the Atlantic coast, just ask for Chalky Mount near Cambridge in St. Joseph parish. There's also **Earth Works Pottery** at Shop Hill in St. Thomas parish where the potters live and work and also serve tea on the veranda of their crafts shop.

For more of a TT-cum-craft shop, there's **Medford Craft Village** in St. Michael parish, which specializes in mahogany carvings, and **Pelican Village,** halfway between Deepwater Cruise Pier and downtown.

Barbados Resources

ANTIQUES

There are a few antique stores around the island, specializing in what British colonists brought over a few hundred years ago, and then some. All require a car, as they are dotted here and there around the island. If you've got the time, or the inclination, check out **Greenwich Antiques,** on the glitter coast at Trent Hill, St. James; **Antiguaria** (near the downtown cruise terminal), Spring Garden Highway, St. Michael; **Antiques & Collectibles,** 15 Pavilion Court, Hastings; and **La Galerie Antique,** Paynes Bay, St. James.

GENERAL STORES

HARRISON'S OF BARBADOS
Broad St., Bridgetown.

The leading duty free and department store of Barbados, with two buildings, Harrison's has good prices on some items and regular duty-free prices on others. They carry all the Eruopean big names in many categories of goods. Harrison's also carries the Lyle and Scott cashmere sweaters, Barrie lambs-wool, Pringle cashmere, and Glen Abbey cashmeres. There is a good selection in Lladro, Kosta Boda, Orrefors, and Christofle. All of the regular china manufacturers you would expect to find are repre-sented as well; beware of low stock.

CAVE SHEPHERD & CO. LTD.
Broad St., Bridgetown.

This is the other department store in town that sells the same things as Harrison's. Their small boutique at the airport sells mostly T-shirts. Founded in 1906 and famous to locals, it's not that impressive to some-one who has been spoiled by the fabulous floating hotels we call cruise ships, with their own boutiques and the duty-free stores that dot the Basin, like Little Switzerland. It's sort of fun and funky, but you could give it a miss and not disappoint me.

There are branch stores dotted around the island; yes, there's one at the cruise terminal.

LITTLE SWITZERLAND
Broad St., Bridgetown.

The Little Switzerland store is divided into two parts because it fits into the street level of the Da Costas Mall. I am a Little Switzerland fan; that's all there is to it.

MALLS

Actually the best of downtown Barbados is located all within one mall, like a pink-frosted cupcake; it's **Da Costas Mall,** which even has a west coast branch in Holetown.

There's also **Sheraton Centre** with about 65 shops at Seargents Village in the parish of Christchurch.

And don't forget the zillions of minimalls that are made up of a clump of chattel-style houses, each a different shop; see a perfect example right at Deep-water Cruise Pier.

Out-of-Town Finds

BATIK CARIBE
Hilton Hotel, Needham's Point.

One of several island-style batik industries (almost every island has one company that represents the island with this kind of work) selling fabric and clothes (and teddy bears, too), all of 100% cotton.

PELICAN VILLAGE

Halfway between where the ships dock and Bridgetown is a small settlement of shops called Pelican Village (☎ 809/427-5350). It was created to sell local craft items, straw-market-type wares, etc.

MOUNT GAY RUM FACTORY

Who cares about submarines that take you to see Davy Jones and all his fish? Who needs boring beaches and stores filled with expensive vases? We need the rum! Take the Mount Gay Luncheon Tour and get a tour of this factory outlet; lunch outdoors under the coconut palms or on the back porch.

You can also just drive by and stop in and shop or tour and shop and have a drink, or two. This great gift shop sells more than rum; charming, wonderful, fun stop.

(Very important: You can also arrange a free ride back and forth from your hotel. Call ☎ 809/435-6900 for reservations and information.)

The factory is on the west coast of the island, not far from the cruise terminal; get your taxi to drop you there and wait, and then continue on along the coast and north toward Speightstown.

Barbados in a Day

The downtown shopping is condensed into one main drag, with the exception of some local art and craft stores near the harbor. You can start from either end of town and return again in under an hour.

If you start from the harbor where the cruise ships dock, you will be walking directly into the craft area, called **Pelican Village.** It is located on Princess Alice Highway, which is all land that has been reclaimed from the sea. Pelican Village has rooms devoted to the different arts and crafts of the island, as well as a fair display of touristy items.

From Pelican Village walk along Princess Alice Highway until you find an appealing street to turn left on. This area of town is mostly warehouses, and you want to get to Lower Broad Street, which turns into Broad Street and is the main drag. Broad Street parallels Princess Alice Highway.

Once on Broad Street, stop into the department stores that cater to the tourist looking for china, crystal, and perfume bargains. There are some unusual selections, but prices are the same here as in other ports. The best place in town to shop is the **Da Costas Mall.**

The local "sell it all" department store is **Cave Shepherd & Co.** You can get the duty-free items along with your sunscreen, booze, and souvenirs.

Broad Street ends at the center of town, Trafalgar Square. Take your hat off to Lord Nelson, whose statue sits in the center of town. From this point you can explore some of the side streets or grab a taxi and head to the Hilton International Barbados, where the shopping center in front offers a concise and air-conditioned version of what you saw in town and where you can sit in the open-air patio by the beach and enjoy a fine flying fish luncheon, alfresco.

If you prefer to explore the northern coast, get a taxi for the half day that's left, and head for the **Mount Gay Rum Factory** where you can tour and eat lunch (alfresco, again), and then explore between Holetown and Speightstown with your taxi driver as your guide—check out **Earthworks Pottery,** the **Sandy Lane Hotel,** and as many mango stands as you can find.

Leave time at the end of your day to shop at **Deepwater Cruise Pier** because this mall is packed with everything you ever wanted to buy anyway.

ANTIGUA

. . . .

Welcome to St. John's

I'm not sure if there really is a town of St. John's or if on Thursday mornings they put it up before the cruise ship comes to town—we did have that late morning arrival.

Is it a mirage, or did the Disney Imagineers stop here first, practicing for what they will do with Disney's own island? This is just a thought, mind you.

Not that St. John's is Disney-perfect, mind you, but therein lies it's charm. St. John's is exactly what you want a Caribbean capital to be.

First off, the ship couldn't dock any closer to town and still be in the water. Second of all, just when you thought you'd seen so much batik you'd never go back into the water, you get an island filled with stores that have real clothes for real people, and even some designer brands.

Stroll off the boat and you are almost immediately inside a store. This is also the first of the Caribbean and designer "name" stores if you are headed upward from Barbados. It's not that the prices are lower than anyplace else; it's that suddenly it's fun to shop again. There's an energy here that you haven't felt on many other islands. This energy leads you into a shopping frenzy. Or maybe it's the sea air.

Warning: this is also the first island of what I call The Diamond Dealers, not just stores that have the word diamond in their names but stores that sell jewelry—diamond, gold, colored gemstones, and more. There are about three major players in the Caribbean; I have no idea how they all stay in business. (Yet I hear that many of them have also opened up in Alaska!)

The basic shopping scene is that this town has at least one of everything: one store for linens from Hong Kong, one branch of **The Athlete's Foot,** one store for Cuban cigars. In many cases, there are several stores selling more or less the same basics—booze, cosmetics, china, and, of course, *tchotchkes.*

Meanwhile, it also has stores that appear to be franchises of big-name shops—**Gucci, Nautica, Tommy Hilfiger, Benetton, Osh Kosh B'Gosh,** and more. I will not say that these stores are frauds, but I personally would not expect that this is the genuine article. I will say that all of these stores make me nervous because I can't quite put my finger on what's right or wrong about them.

The Gucci store is the most confusing in this respect, but I'd swear this is not the Gucci from Italy that I know and love. I'd also swear that I will love the handbag I bought for $165 until I die, even if it's fake Gucci.

Antigua Resources
Body & Bath

🛍 The Body Shop
Heritage Quay.

You could have knocked me over with a tea tree when I saw The Body Shop's traditional dark green storefront in Antigua—possibly the first store I saw as I got off the boat. The store is indeed a Body Shop with an extra plus; in the rear is a very good gift shop. I think the store next door actually merged into the space. The combination of the two stores and The Body Shop's "save the whales" philosophy just works together like a symphony.

Selection wise, the store has just about everything you expect, except for the little travel sizes. Price wise, the values actually vary. Some items were a few dollars less than in the U.S., others were a little bit more. All items are marked with two price stickers, the price in EC and the price in U.S. dollars.

CARIBBEAN STYLE

ISLAND TREASURES
St. Mary's St.

This is a TT (tourist trap); I don't deny it. But I think they have a good selection and fair prices on the usual junk plus many items that were a little bit special: potholders made out of jazzy Caribbean fabrics, many tin painted items, a line of frige magnets called Clay Critters, and more. Worth a browse.

DECIBELS
Redcliffe Quay.

Most of the goods in this store are imported from Mexico, but the store just has a contemporary air to it and doesn't feel like a fiesta. There's lots of tin, some pottery, and some glass along with a few other items for tourists. I've never seen a handmade mermaid doll before, and this one was adorable.

JACARANDA
Redcliffe St.

From the street, this store may not look like your kind of place. I was afraid it was going to be just another head shop but was thrilled to get inside and see not only style and classy local items but many items from the Sunny Caribbee line, which I had first discovered in San Juan. Best buy: soap packaged in a small bag, printed with the firm's logo for $5. Many other Caribbean delights as well.

CIGARS

LA CASA DEL HABANO
Heritage Quay.

Romeo, Romeo wherefore art thou? He's managing a cigar shop in the West Indies love, care for a smoke? Romeo is indeed the managing director of this shop and stresses that this is a chain that stands behind its selection and its quality, cautioning me that there are tons of counterfeits out there.

This is very much a guy's kind of shop; few women even venture in. Although the store asks for your name at the time of the sale for the duty-free records), many men balk at giving their real name and simply say John Doe . . . or Count of Monte Cristo. The store and the selection are pretty large; the product is Cuban, and it is illegal to bring Cuban cigars back into the U.S.

FASHION

BLACK & WHITE
High St.

You won't have any trouble finding this store, it's white with black polka dots all over the front. I expected that it would only sell black-and-white clothing but was wrong—there were wonderful cotton gauze droopy dresses à la Eileen Fisher ($78) and then silks and knits and many cutting-edge styles for the Mod Squad.

NOREEN PHILIPPS
Redcliffe Quay.

With the promise of couture posted out front, this store sells casual and dress-up clothes perfect for any event on a cruise ship. Most of the dressy styles were too beaded and fussy for my taste, but the store will make up any garment you want in about 2 hours. There was a silk suit that caught my fancy, but at almost $400, I can wait for the Calvin Klein sale.

A THOUSAND FLOWERS
Redcliffe St.

This store is crammed with resort wear, most of it not the batiky Caribe stuff but rather linen or flax and flowy. It's chic and wearable in hot weather anyplace in the world, not just in the islands. Prices are moderate, but there are no bargains; most dresses cost $75 to $95. Mostly brands that are also sold in the U.S.; another Eileen Fisher kind of place.

KRIZIA
Heritage Quay.

Okay, so Miucci designs the Krizia line in Milan; but she owns a resort on the nearby island of Barbuda (K club), so she opened a store in town, but no one could afford to buy anything. Gee, I wonder why.

So the store kept its name but evolved into an affordable fashions store, selling brands such as Kenar and looks that are great for a resort and the real world—a hard combination. They have good sales, and if you buy a lot, the co-partner in the firm, Natalie, will help you round down the price a little bit. Really classy and elegant clothes, carefully chosen by a good eye.

BASE
Redcliffe Quay.

If Giorgio Armani started out in the West Indies, he might have come up with this: beige knit T-shirts, all chicer than thou but costing $85, which is no particular bargain, especially since the goods are made in Antigua. There's also a kids' line and there's a few gift items such as picture frames, which are lovely—rough-hewn wood, hand-painted and faded, with metal doodads, at $25 each. Expensive but chic, like everything else here.

FASHIONDOCK
Heritage Quay.

I wish I could give you the real lowdown on this store, which sells Gianni Versace and a line called Johnny Heaven. The shop has a wide range of Versace items from different Versace lines,

including Versus—prices on most items are in line
with what Versace should be: $90 for a tie, $350
for a beach towel. However, I bought a pair of thongs
in Versace printed stretch lycra that I've never seen
in the line and makes me wonder just how genuine
they are. They were marked down from $70, but
my notion is not one of price, it's simply of charac-
ter. However, the shoes are so fabulous I don't care
if they are real or fake, and I wouldn't even give
them to Donatella if she asked for them.

JEWELRY

THE GOLD SMITTY
Redcliffe Quay.

As much as I basically hate all jewelry shops in the
Caribbean, I kind of like this one. It feels good to
walk in—it's large and low-key, and the styles are
of a certain kind but don't look like they came from
last year's *Spiegel* catalog.

MALLS

HERITAGE QUAY SHOPPING CENTRE
Heritage Quay.

All coral stucco with turquoise railings, this two
story mall is in the block right after The Body Shop
and is the heart of the downtown shopping district.
This is the prime real estate and where the better
known stores, such as **Little Switzerland,** are located.
Clean bathrooms; pay phones.

REDCLIFFE QUAY

This isn't actually a mall, but since other guidebooks
say it is, I don't want to confuse you too much. This
is a group of warehouses and stores with streetfront
addresses and then courtyard addresses and lots of
opportunity for some fabulous Caribbean-style
photography. In the courtyard there are little cottages turned into stores, each painted in charming
colors—some with flowers and vines.

Chapter Twelve

· · · · · · · · · · ·

THE MEXICAN CARIBBEAN: CANCÚN, COZUMEL, TULUM, XEL-HA & MÉRIDA

CARIBBEAN MEXICO

· ·

The first time I set foot on the island of Cozumel, I walked around dumbfounded—this is the best of the Caribbean, I kept thinking . . . and it's Mexico! I was on a cruise that had included the Cayman Islands and a stop in Jamaica, neither of which were shopping ports. Cozumel filled me with delight and wonder.

Indeed, if you simply look at a map, you can see that the sweep of Mexico brings part of it right into the Caribbean Sea. Furthermore, tourism officials in Mexico have been developing the area in order to satisfy cruise passengers and are developing more and more facilities; Mérida is the latest target city for more improvements for cruise passengers.

So come on down to a very special part of the world, another type of Caribbean blend that is not French, Dutch, or British but still very much in the spirit of the melting pot. Mexico could well be the best shopping destination you visit while on board.

The part of Mexico that borders the Caribbean is dramatically different from the rest of the country, partly because of a difference in climate and topography (the coastline is almost entirely jungle, and the terrain of the interior, with the exception of a mountainous region along the border of the Yucatán state, is surprisingly flat), but mainly because of a difference in culture. Unlike the rest of Mexico, which was settled by Spaniards, the people who settled this region were mostly blacks from the West Indies. As a result, the culture is influenced more by Africa than by Spain.

A trip to Caribbean Mexico is much more like a trip to the islands. As in the islands, there are resort communities, some of which, like Cancún, were developed under a government-sponsored initiative. But there are also far less developed beachfront towns that respond, as they have for hundreds of years, more to the rhythm of the surf than the wristwatch. And, of course, there's shopping everywhere.

In the interior, you add a world of archaeological digs and ruins to the mix, and even more incredible shopping. In fact, the shopping here is better than elsewhere in the Caribbean.

The Lay of the Land

The Yucatán boot has three primary advantages over the rest of the world: gorgeous beaches (with luxury resorts to match); mysterious and fascinating ruins; and two types of shopping experiences: tourist-style, as in Cancún and Cozumel, and native style, as in Mérida.

Cancún has a lot going for it, but it's too over developed for me. I nonetheless have to admire its Miami Beach–style hotels and resorts and its fabulous location. And unlike many Caribbean resorts, there's plenty to see and do here, much of which is multigenerational: I've been here with my son, my father, and my photographer, and each of us found different things to enjoy. But the bay is too shallow for cruise ships, so it becomes a long schlep for a day-trip, although it is offered by most ships that come to the area.

CANCÚN

. . . .

You have to love Cancún the minute you walk through the airport upon arrival: No other Caribbean airport has as many shops. As you depart in a van (far cheaper than a taxi) crammed with other gringos, you'll see giant billboards tucked into the dunes, advertising the Ralph Lauren shop and other in-town stores. What's not to like?

Cancún may be commercial and glitzy and very, very American, but it welcomes you with *abrazos* (hugs) and a lot of air-conditioned malls. Cancún may be overbuilt, similar to Las Vegas and filled to the grains of sand with gringos, but it's got a fabulous location and offers days packed with activity (sports and shopping and culture, too!) and nights filled with many dining choices. So welcome to Cancún, a little bit of America in Mexico, where the water in the sink is safe and the water in the sea is fabulous. Welcome to Cancún, where shopping isn't a chore, it's part of the scenery.

Cancún on a Cruise

A few years ago some cruise ships put in at Cancún, which meant they got as close to Cancún as they could and then tendered passengers to shore. There is no pier in Cancún itself, and the waters do not provide for a close anchorage, so the launch ride was about an hour. Needless to say, this wasn't popular.

Nowadays, most cruise ships stop at Playa del Carmen and offer a day tour to Cancún for those who want to visit. Unfortunately, the ship usually then moves on to Cozumel, so you are forced to pick between three different spots: Playa del Carmen, Cancún, or Cozumel.

If your ship's itinerary is unclear, you might want to have all this explained to you. Many passengers think they are going to all three cities. Also note that if you are on a cruise that offers a tour of the archaeological ruins at Tulum, you will not get to visit any of the other choices. There is some shopping in the parking lot at Tulum, but not a lot.

The Two Cancúns

If you're staying in one of the popular resort hotels, you're in an area called the Hotel Zone, a strip of land in the shape of the number seven that's attached to the mainland at both ends. In the top left-hand corner of the number seven is Cancún City. This is the mainland and where smaller (and less-expensive) hotels are located.

As you cross onto the "seven" away from Cancún City, you'll work your way through the famed hotel area, where a narrow strip of land with beach on both sides plays host to some of the most glorious resorts you have ever seen. At the bottom of the seven, you connect to the portion of land that leads to the airport and to Club Med.

In the beginning, when Cancún was first developed—more than 20 years ago—the center of the Hotel Zone was considered to be at the break in the number seven, where the top zigs and then plunges downward; this is an area of town known as Caracol. Today, it's where you'll find the Old Convention Center, the main shopping areas, and the Hotel Camino Real. It used to be where all the hotels and resorts were located, but as Cancún has become more and more popular, hotels have been built all along the seven. At one time the Sheraton was considered at the end of the world. Now, hotels reach almost to the airport at the end of the seven.

Developers are already trying to move the so-called center of town away from Caracol and farther along the neck of the seven, across the street from the Sheraton where México Mágico and the New Convention Center are.

Getting Around

You are most likely to be visiting with a motor coach and a tour. Nonetheless, you can do this independently.

By Bus No matter where you're staying in Cancún, you can get around inexpensively on the Zona Hoteler'a shuttle bus. These buses simply travel up and down the hotel strip, stopping at each hotel's driveway. Flag one down, and the driver will allow you to board. Just make sure the bus is traveling in the direction you're headed! These are luxury coaches, not Joan Wilder–type buses.

By Taxi Taxis can be flagged down with ease in downtown Cancún City; many are metered. It's harder to flag down a taxi yourself in the hotel zone, but your hotel, or restaurant, will gladly call one for you. Taxis that linger in front of hotels usually have English-speaking drivers, but higher prices.

By Car When I visit Cancún, I usually rent a car. For my last trip, I reserved a car from the U.S. with automatic transmission, air-conditioning, and a cassette player. When I arrived in Cancún to pick up the car, I did not end up with the car I'd reserved, and I'd paid more than the agreed-upon price. While it all worked out fine in the end, it taught me a valuable lesson about renting cars in Mexico: What you reserve and what you get can be two very different things.

Do not expect the process of renting a car in Mexico to be hassle-free, regardless of the firm you use. Reserve a car from the U.S. before you depart. Even though you might not get what you asked for, you'll get a car. If you wait until you arrive, you may not. Be prepared to fight for your rights, and have your paperwork with you. But in the end, expect to compromise. I don't think it's really worth it for a cruise passenger to rent a car on a one-day basis.

About Addresses

Please note that while Cancún City has street addresses and is based on a grid system, there are few addresses on the strip since everything is situated along the long Kukulcán Boulevard that's sometimes called Boulevard Cancún.

Most stores are located in either hotels or shopping centers, all of which have names. There are numbered markers for each kilometer as you work your way down the strip from town, and you'll soon learn that kilometer 3.5 (the address given for Plaza Nautilus, a shopping center) is rather close to Cancún City, whereas kilometer 12, the address of the Sheraton, is rather far from Cancún City.

Most directions are given based upon their proximity to a particular hotel. For example, you may be told, "It's just past the Fiesta Americana." Street numbers are not usually included in an address or a set of directions.

Landlubber's Delight

🛍 Ritz-Carlton Cancún
Blvd. Kukulcán, Retorno del Rey 36. ☎ *800/ 241-3333 in the U.S., or 98/850-808; fax 98/851-015.*

Although it looks like a giant pink fortress from the road, the Ritz-Carlton Cancún lives up to its famous name once you pull up to the lobby— Mexican rococo is the style of the day and it is sumptuous. There's something delightful about being in a pair of shorts and a T-shirt amid French antiques, gilt mirrors, and Persian carpets. And the views from its public areas are phenomenal! There's nothing better than eating outside on the patio under an umbrella. The banana pancakes aren't bad, either. Rooms face either the lagoon or the ocean. The shopping within the hotel itself is limited; there's a branch of **Escada** and a few other upscale stores. The real hit is the **Ritz-Carlton gift shop.** It sells what may be the best beach-related logo merchandise you've ever seen!

CASA TURQUESA
Blvd. Kukulcán, 13.5km. ☏ *98/852-925; fax 98/852-922.*

One of the most expensive hotels in Cancún, Casa Turquesa is a secret hideaway for the well heeled. A small hotel with only 31 rooms, all of which are suites, it overlooks the ocean and resembles a colonial mansion. It may have the most unique setting in all of Cancún. It's built around a pool and is situated next door to a terrific shopping mall.

HOTEL CAMINO REAL
Blvd. Kukulcán, 5km. ☏ *800/223-6800 or 98/830-100; fax 98/832-965.*

As elsewhere in Mexico, the Camino Real is one of the toniest hotels in town. It has a great location right at the tip of Caracol and super shopping in its own virtual mall (there are stores that sell crafts and costume jewelry, and there's a salon). At the time of writing, I was looking at packages to Cancún and saw that this hotel (a member of Leading Hotels of the World) was included in one of the least expensive packages offered. If the same is true when you're researching your trip, this is a terrific value.

Snack & Shop

Below, a few tidbits:

- All American fast-food chains have a branch in Cancún. If you're worried about what's safe to eat, or have kids with you who want food from home, KFC is spoken here.
- Malls have tons of places to eat; you can snack and shop your way across the hotel zone.
- I prefer to snack my way through the hotel zone while inspecting hotels—I eat lunch at a

different hotel every day. My favorite hotel restaurants for lunch are anywhere in the **Ritz-Carlton** (both the patio and the indoor dining room are great for either breakfast or lunch) and **Azulejos,** the cafe at the Camino Real.

Shopping Cancún

Cancún is not the best shopping city in Mexico, or even in the Yucatán, nor is it the cheapest; so you are indeed shopping for the fun of it here. And since most items in Mexico aren't too expensive anyway, it doesn't really matter if you could have done better at the Indian market on Friday in Toluca. Toluca is 1,000 miles away. If you have to pick a single day trip while your ship lies at anchor, Cancún is not the shopping day—Cozumel is.

Best Buys of Cancún

Cancún may not have the best shopping on the Yucatán peninsula, but there are several items that qualify as best buys there.

CIGARS

You can't bring them back home with you (if you live in the U.S.), but you can certainly light up on your vacation. You can get Havana cigars at many tobacco shops in Cancún, but the best is **Casa del Habano** in Flamingo Plaza.

SEÑOR FROG'S T-SHIRTS

For $10, these make great gifts for teenagers. (I even bought one for a French hotelier friend of mine.)

WATER BOTTLES

Just as at Walt Disney World, Cancún has tons of those plastic water bottles with a plastic straw attached. I think the most attractive one of all is sold at the Ritz-Carlton's gift shop on the lower level of the hotel. It costs $6 and comes in pristine white with the hotel's logo in royal blue. Very status-y.

Cancún Resources

BIG NAMES

ACA JOE
Plaza Caracol, Hotel Zone; Avenida Tulum, Cancún City; Airport.

The Mexican equivalent of The Gap, Aca Joe has several shops in Cancún. Their stuff isn't dirt cheap, but it is moderately priced and well designed.

GUCCI
Plaza Caracol, Hotel Zone; Plaza Flamingo, Hotel Zone.

This store is nice and the merchandise can be, too, but check each piece individually to be sure it's well made. Prices are about 30% less than in the U.S., and the goods are genuine Gucci, but the quality is iffy. You can buy a sensational pair of loafers for $100, but you won't find the new Gucci that's taking the world by storm.

POLO/RALPH LAUREN
Plaza Caracol, Hotel Zone.

Here's where you can buy Polo clothes for men, women, and children at a fraction of their U.S. prices. That's not to say they're giving things away: A shirt costs about $45.

DUTY-FREE SHOPPING

ULTRA FEMME
Plaza Caracol, Hotel Zone; Avenida Tulum, Cancún City.

The best, and glitziest, duty-free shop in town, Ultra Femme has branches in various malls and on the main shopping street in Cancún City. This store is so sophisticated, it publishes its own four-color booklet (complete with perfume ads, natch) that compares its prices with U.S. retail prices.

The firm has been going strong for 20 years, about as long as Cancún has been buzzing. In addition to perfume and beauty products, there are accessories (but no Hermès scarves) and even Rolex watches.

I found the savings real but minimal on most items (about $3). I find I can get greater savings shopping mail order from the U.S. If you are visiting from England or Europe, you may be more impressed with the savings, however.

On the other hand, the stores are among the most fun to shop in Cancún and are certainly the most glamorous. They are also air-conditioned, which is a blessing in the heat. There are a total of 10 boutiques in Cancún, but I've only listed the addresses of the two most convenient branches above. I like the one in Plaza Caracol best. Many languages are spoken; the salespeople are eager and savvy. And every now and then, you may even catch a bargain. Stores open at 10am daily.

MARKETS

Cancún's markets are very touristy, but they're still fun.

KI HUIC
Ave. Tulum, Cancún City.

Located in Cancún City, this market is a mass of stalls selling souvenirs. In season, the prices are better than on the strip. (Silver is 85¢ a gram here, 95¢ in the hotel zone, and $1 in malls.) You should bargain, of course, and don't pay more than $8 for one of those blankets ($6 is better). *Note:* Many of the vendors observe the siesta and are closed in the afternoon.

The motor coach crowd may think this is Mexico, but you and I know better.

Plaza Coral Negro
Hotel Zone, 9.5km.

I don't care if this is a tourist trap; I don't care if the vendors can spot you from 3,000 miles away. I happen to love this market. How can you not love a market that's painted hot pink?

Located in the hotel zone, near the Convention Center, this *tianguis* (flea market) is laid out like a California strip mall. A series of connecting tile avenues are lined with rows of vendors and dozens of places to sit (there's even a fountain). If you look hard enough, you'll find a very nice, small shrine to the Virgin Mary. Vendors hang out their doorways, trying to entice you to buy by saying outrageous things. "Hey, missus, you buy here real cheap. I give you good deal. I know your husband is watching your bucks."

Some of the vendors are seriously good, such as Martha, whereas others are just liquor stores that sell tequila and chips. The atmosphere is decidedly different from the border town feel of the market downtown. If you have limited time for shopping, this is the only stop you need to make in town. (I've got others out of town, trust me.)

SHOPPING CENTERS

Plaza Caracol
Hotel Zone, 8km.

This is the big daddy of shopping centers on Cancún's resort strip. It's not the oldest, or the newest—it's simply the biggest and the fanciest. If you only "do" one mall, this is the one. It has a strange shape and several entrances and faces both the lagoon and the beach. There are about 200 shops in the mall, many of which are designer names.

Among others, you'll find branches of **Aca Joe, Ralph Lauren / Polo, Ultra Femme, Benetton,** and **Gucci.** For something more original, try **Galerías Coloniales** (crafts and Pier 1–style merchandise), **Tane** (an exclusive jeweler and silversmith), and **Las Sandías** (papier-mâché products). Open daily 8am to 10pm. Some stores close for the siesta from 1 to 4pm.

KUKULCÁN PLAZA
Hotel Zone, 13km.

This shopping center is next door to Casa Turquesa, near the Fiesta Americana. It's a new, very glitzy mall but, to me, it doesn't have any soul. There's a **Señor Frog's** retail store, a branch of every T-shirt chain store, and a few other upscale yuppie stores, but this isn't the best mall in town. Open daily 9am to 10pm.

PLAZA LAGUNAS
Hotel Zone, 8.5km (next to Plaza Caracol).

This shopping center is hard to distinguish from the jumble of shops crowded into the Plaza Caracol area. Its look can be described as jungle-lodge-meets-parking garage. If that doesn't help, look for the Kentucky Fried Chicken—it's right next door. The two reasons to shop here are **Calvin Klein** and **Ellesse.** The **Hard Rock Café** is around the back. Open daily 9am to 10pm.

INTERPLAZA
Hotel Zone, 9km (Convention Center).

The new kid in town, InterPlaza is still under development. It was built as part of the new Convention Center to offer convention goers easy access to the big names of local shopping; 40 stores. Open daily 9am to 10pm.

PLAZA NAUTILUS
Hotel Zone, 3.5km.

This one sticks out like a sore thumb because of its adventurous architecture, which is really saying something considering the bizarre look of most of Cancún's malls. Plaza Nautilus vies with Plaza Caracol for the title of most upscale mall in Cancún. At kilometer 3.5, it's the closest strip shopping center to Cancún City and is situated next door to the hottest disco in town, **La Boom.** What an evening *paseo* (stroll): Shop all evening, walk next door, check your bags, and boogie all night. Open daily 9am to 10pm.

FLAMINGO PLAZA
Hotel Zone, 11km.

I call the style of this mall's architecture Aztec Adorable. All the shops have been fitted into a semi-prefab, pyramid-style strip mall overlooking the lagoon, not far from the Sheraton. Most of the stores are branches of established names such as **Bye-Bye** and **Gucci,** but there's also the usual plethora of silver shops. Nothing to write home about, but convenient for those who are staying nearby. Open daily 9am to 9pm.

PLAZA LA FIESTA
Hotel Zone, 9km.

Plaza la Fiesta isn't exactly a shopping center, even though it bills itself as one. While many locals call giant indoor stores like this an indoor *tianguis,* in all honesty, Plaza la Fiesta is nothing more than a department store that sells touristy souvenirs— Kmart-meets-Cancún, if you will. The huge space has aisle after aisle brimming with crafts, liquor, leather goods, and dresses. There are also swarms of people. Getting the picture? This place is a lot like downtown St. Thomas on a day when three cruise ships come into port. A mariachi band plays in the front of the shop, music blares, money flashes. There's even a photo opportunity out front. Open daily 9am to 9pm.

SILVER

🛍 SOQUI
Plaza Caracol 2, Hotel Zone.

Of the zillions of silver shops in Cancún, and even in this mall, this one stands bangle and earrings above the rest. One of the reasons I like it is because there are items you don't see elsewhere, including sterling silver perfume bottles with gemstone tops (around $75).

I once fell in love with a double length, magnificent silver ball necklace for which I bargained very fiercely. I let it go in the end, but of all the silver necklaces in the entire country, this one was the best—and the price, $300, was more or less fair.

There are also lots of fashion earrings that don't look like cheap souvenirs, tea sets, and various serving pieces in silver.

🛍 RONAY
Plaza Caracol, Hotel Zone.

One of the most famous big-name jewelers in town (the other is Tane), selling top-of-the-line works and expensive but important silver.

SEBASTIAN
Plaza Caracol 1; Plaza Caracol 2; Plaza Nautilus.

This famous maker also has stores in Oaxaca and Taxco; I usually shop at one of the two branches in Plaza Caracol.

COZUMEL

. . . .

Olé! Now this is a shopping day! Hey Hey!

As un-Mexican as Cancún is, Cozumel is a totally different experience. Not that it's more Mexican, mind you. It's actually more Caribbean. Cozumel is Mexico's largest Caribbean Island. Even though it's 28 miles long and 11 miles wide, it's only 3% developed, with vast stretches of jungle and uninhabited shoreline. It's fun, it's alive, it's casual, and it affords a chance to go a little native.

Cozumel is host to the Palancar Reef, one of the best places in the world to go diving or snorkeling and see some beautiful tropical fish. Because all the stores close for a hearty siesta, an organized day-tripper or cruise passenger on shore leave can fit in both some shopping and some snorkeling.

On my last day trip, I did a little shopping in town, then I drove into the jungle past the Meliá Hotel and spent a few marvelous moments listening to the sounds of the earth while spotting crabs and pretending to be a wild adventurer (do note that your car rental insurance is null and void the minute you leave the paved road). Afterward, I had drinks on the beach at the Meliá and a lobster in a hut across the street. What a perfect day . . . and it was one day, perfect for a cruise passenger as well.

Getting There

Some cruise ships list the port of call as Playa del Carmen and then let passengers make their own way to the various area treats, including Cozumel. In that case, you hop the ferry. There are fast ferries, slow ferries, cats, and hydrofoils from Playa del Carmen to Cozumel. I call them all "the ferry." There's also a car ferry that departs for Cozumel from Puerto Morelos. But as I don't recommend it (it's difficult to drive around Cozumel); this section just covers the passenger ferry. In order to catch the passenger ferry, you must get yourself from Cancún to the seaside port town of Playa del Carmen.

There are two different ferry companies. One is faster (and more expensive) than the other, despite the fact that both tell you they take the same amount of time to get there.

If you are spending the day in Cozumel and want to take the last ferry back to Playa del Carmen, verify what time it leaves when you arrive. To be safe, verify it twice—as you're departing Playa del Carmen and as you arrive in Cozumel. With two different companies running boats, there are two different last times!

Arriving in Cozumel

Please note that the ferry from Playa del Carmen arrives at a different pier than the one used by cruise ships. The ferry arrives at a pier right in the heart of downtown.

If you arrive via cruise ship, you will probably take a launch to the International Cruise Pier, about 2 miles from downtown.

Getting Around

All of Cozumel's shopping is situated in two compact areas, near the ferry pier. They sit side by side and can easily be managed by foot, even on a hot day.

If you come to Cozumel via cruise ship, you'll need to take a taxi or a van into town if you want to shop there. Taxi fares are usually calculated per person, in U.S. dollars.

If you hail a taxi downtown with the intention of going to the cruise ship pier or a hotel, ask the driver the price before you get in, and make sure you both agree on the currency in which the price is to be paid. Also make sure the agreed-upon fare is for all members of your party. Don't assume you are paying $2 for the complete fare, and you won't be surprised when it turns out to be $2 per person.

If you come into the main pier in the heart of downtown, where the ferries from Playa del Carmen dock, you can walk everywhere and will not need any other transportation unless you want to go to the reefs or a far-flung lobster restaurant or you want a tour of the island.

On my last visit with Ian, I fell in love with the notion of renting a jeep and tooling around the island. Unfortunately, I didn't get this notion until we were halfway across the bay and on our way to Cozumel, and I mistakenly thought you could walk into any car rental agency, flash a credit card, and get a jeep. I also thought car rental would be about $35 a day. Wrong. Jeep rental is $65 a day; jeeps are often rented with empty gas tanks, and the only gas pump on the island is downtown. Despite the fact that we only had the car for 2 to 3 hours, it was still fun, but renter beware! Your ship can arrange a rental for you, or your travel agent can do it before you arrive.

The Lay of the Land

The big city on Cozumel is San Miguel. It's also the only city. It's laid out on a simple grid system with one additional street: Avenida Rafael Melgar, which is the main drag along the beach that goes around the island. This street from the pier north is called, as it is on any island, the *malecón,* or seawall. The new snappy shops are along the *malecón,* all sitting in a row on one side of the street.

The other shopping area, which is more the style of Old Mexico Meets Cute Turista, begins at the *zócalo* (town square), which is where you get off the main pier or where the cruise van takes you. It continues alongside the *zócalo* on what I call Fifth Avenue. The real name of this street is Calle 5, and it has a north end *(norte)* and a south end *(sur)* divided by Avenida Benito Juárez (a pedestrian street), which is where the *zócalo* is. This part of town is far more funky, has the better crafts shops, and gives you much more of the flavor of Mexico. However, the beauty of Cozumel (aside from the fish in the sea) is that the shopping is 500% better than in Cancún.

If you arrive on a cruise ship, this is the big day, folks—this is Shopping Day. If you are on the "western Caribbean" swing, you'll note that shopping in the Caymans is far more expensive and in Jamaica it is, well, more native. Cozumel is where you can buy a little of everything from wearable ready-to-wear to Mexican arts and crafts. Cozumel is just about the most perfect one-day shopping adventure you can have.

Cruising Choices

If you are on a cruise that makes you choose among three destinations for your day trip—Playa del Carmen for the Tulum all-day trip, Cancún, or Cozumel—and you are making this decision solely based on how good the shopping is, I suggest you pick Cozumel. Here's why:

- Cancún has a bunch of shopping centers that are a lot like what you're used to at home. While they have a lot of everything, everything is extremely resorty and doesn't offer you much of the feel or look of the real Mexico.
- Playa del Carmen's shopping was all created for tourists and there's not much of it.
- Tulum, while a fascinating archaeological site, has a *tianguis* that's just one giant rip-off. The best of this region's shopping is actually at Xel-Ha (see page 247).
- Cozumel has its share of tourist joints, but it also has a degree of charm that is equal to any other Caribbean port. You can also get a better selection of crafts here and have more fun shopping for them than in other cities. Yes, there is some

shopping in the international terminal for cruise passengers.

Cruisers' Warning

My friend CB went to Cozumel on a cruise, took the launch to the pier, the taxi to town, shopped till stores closed, took a taxi back to the cruise pier, took the launch back to the ship, and ate lunch with her family on board the ship. Then, late in the afternoon, she repeated the process. With all this, she still didn't get to one of the main shopping areas because she discovered it too late in her day.

Shopping Neighborhoods

Even though the town of San Miquel is small, it has a few hidden secrets. You may want to carry a map with you so you're sure to find all the areas worth shopping.

Malecón

Avenida Raphael Melgar is the official name of the street that runs along the waterfront of Cozumel and is known as *The Malecón*. It begins just about where the ferries from Playa del Carmen arrive and stretches for a few blocks to your left, if you are facing the *malecón* and the water is to your rear. This is where the most expensive stores in Cozumel are located, including the famous **Polo / Ralph Lauren** and the infamous **Van Cleef and Arpels**.

Fifth Avenue

Actually, this street's name is Calle 5. It's where you'll find some of those hidden treasures I promised. To acclimate yourself, check a map. When you do, you'll see that downtown Cozumel is a grid, with Avenida Juárez at its center. The streets are numbered, as are the alternating cross-streets. I call this whole area

Hidden Downtown, and the best part is the crafts market at Calle Sur 1. It's not the best crafts market ever, but now you know. Fifth Avenue is more fun— pedestrian street of tourist traps and cafes.

MALECÓN SUR

Below the *Malecón* is the waterfront road that leads to the snorkeling beaches. There is some shopping along this street, especially in the southern blocks right off the square. The addresses of these shops are usually written *Maelcón Sur,* and they tend to be mini-department stores and so-called duty-free shops.

Store Hours

For a big-time shopping port, Cozumel has a terrible secret: Lots of places close for the siesta! Not all of them, but a fair number. Stores hours are basically 9am to 1pm and 5 to 9pm daily. Do your most important shopping first thing off.

Black Coral Shopping

All those black-coral factory outlets you see (or are taken to on your tour bus) are not real factories. Well, they are real factories, but they aren't real factory outlets. There are no bargains. In fact, this is rip-off city. I don't suggest you go for black coral in a big way, since it's very hard to distinguish the real thing from black plastic, and few makers craft fashion pieces—just little touristy items. Price carefully, and if you are a serious shopper, buy from a reputable source.

Best Buys of Cozumel

Cozumel has several items that can be considered best buys.

Arts & Crafts

Cozumel sells crafts from various regions of Mexico at stores all over. There's a far better selection than in Cancún.

Vanilla

Vanilla is sold in bottles of various sizes, and yes, it's the real thing. At $4 a bottle, it's a great inexpensive souvenir. You may have to declare it as part of your liquor allowance in some states, however.

About Those Stores

I don't need to tell you that the store called Van Cleef and Arpels is in no way related to the famous international jeweler of the same name.

I don't need to tell you that there are a million tourist traps, T-shirt shops (and factory outlets), and crafts bazaars the likes of which you've already had the opportunity to shop in Cancún. (**La Fiesta** has three locations right on the waterfront!)

I shouldn't need to tell you that there is a **Carlos 'N' Charlie's** in town and that they sell T-shirts and logo merchandise there. They are open every day except Sunday from 9am to 2am; on Sundays they don't open until noon. If you've never heard of this food-and-drink chain, now could be the time to get a little firsthand knowledge. It's located on the *malecón,* right near the center of town.

About Those Gems

My girlfriend MaryAnn was recently visiting Cozumel via cruise ship and stopped into the fanciest of the jewelry stores, where she was terrified to learn that colored stones are being touted as "African Emeralds," which sounds awfully nice but is meaningless. Any gemstone that comes with a qualifier means that it's not what you want it to be.

Finds

Poco-Loco
Plaza Studebaker (Malecón at Calle 2).

This is one of those Mexican chain stores that pops up in every resort city—sort of the local equivalent of The Gap or Banana Republic. Their graphics are a little different from Bye-Bye (their main competitor) and are de rigueur with the tourist crowd.

Polo/Ralph Lauren
Ave. Rafael Melgar 11 (Malecón at Calle 4).

On my last visit, I was insulted to discover that not everything here was cheap: They have the nerve to sell dresses for $100! You just have to realize that prices here are still 30% to 50% of what they are in the U.S. and not get too greedy. Then you can cope. This is one of the nicest Ralph Lauren stores you'll see in all of Mexico.

Los Cinco Soles
Ave. Rafael Melgar 27 (Malecón at Calle 8).

This is my favorite shop in Cozumel and the only one you need to visit if you're in a hurry. It's toward the end of the shopping part of the *malecón*, so head here first, and then work your way back to town. It's in an old colonial building; every room (salon, really) is filled with arts and crafts. Even the postcards are better than anywhere else.

True, this is a glorified tourist shop, but their selection of Mexican glass is excellent. There are lots of clothes for kids, and they sell vanilla.

Pama
Ave. Rafael Melgar Sur, No. 9.

This is a branch of a local department store. It's new and modern and looks like a duty-free shop at any world airport. Since Cozumel is, like Cancún, a duty-free port, you may want to price various objects you need to stock up on. As I mentioned in the Cancún section, I didn't find any great bargains, but Pama does carry all the big brands. Note that while most of the stores on this street are located to the left of the *zócalo,* Pama is located to the right.

ACA JOE
Ave. Rafael Melgar (Malecón at Calle 6).

This is yet another branch of the same store you'll find in every Mexican resort. But if you haven't been to an Aca Joe yet, this could be your favorite store in town. There's no crossover with the merchandise Aca Joe sells in the U.S., but it's a great store nonetheless.

TULUM & XEL-HA

· ·

Your ship will undoubtedly offer excursions to either Tulum or Xel-Ha. Here's a quick rundown of your shopping ops while on these excursions.

Tulum   After a quick tramp through the bushes in Tulum, and a good hard stare at the sea and one of the most breathtaking vistas of any of Mexico's ruins, head back to the shopping area, which is set up like a *tianguis* (flea market). Here you'll find two separate rows of corrugated tin stalls from which vendors sell souvenirs. If you thought the ruins were something, consider the prices here. Yes, they're ruinous!

There is no question that the asking price on silver pieces in Tulum is more than 100% inflated and would be high for Tiffany & Co., let alone any other U.S. retailer. Unless you are willing to bargain and possibly walk away or overspend dramatically, you should not buy silver in Tulum. A chunky silver bracelet I saw in Cancún for $125 (a price well researched and bargained for) was offered for sale in Tulum for $350.

The only thing for which you will not overpay in Tulum is a bottle of Coca-Cola (or Krystal water) you buy when you finish exploring the ruins. After a morning in the hot sun, it's one item that's worth any price!

Xel-Ha   Much better shopping! This is simply one of the best places in Mexico. Technically, Xel-Ha is a game reserve for fish. There's a small museum here, several snack bars where you will certainly want to sit down and have a cold beer or a Coke, and places to go snorkeling.

Without a doubt, your best buy in Xel-Ha will be the $1 you spend on fish food to make the brilliantly colored fish swim right up beside you, but you'll also enjoy the great values in silver, T-shirts, and other souvenirs.

MÉRIDA

Only a few cruise ships now offer passengers the opportunity to visit Mérida, but this port is opening up because it offers a look at a still authentic part of the real Mexico. I can't oversell Mérida as the best place on earth; it was oversold to me, and I was heartbroken. But if you're ready for something real and very funky, *vaya te*.

Mérida is the capital of the state of Yucatán, so yes, at last you are in the Yucatán. It's the main market city for not only the state but for the entire boot of Mexico, and for those as far south as Belize. Some airlines fly to Mérida not only from the Mexican interior, but from southern points in the U.S.

Mérida's colonial history includes both French and Lebanese settlers, so the city has many buildings with mansard roofs and a style of architecture not usually seen in Mexico. A lot of the buildings date from the mid-1500s (the cathedral was built in 1598, but the Montejo home—now a museum—dates from 1549). There's also a large parklike plaza, or *zócalo,* and a well-attended evening *paseo.* This is a city with a large population and a lot of commerce.

More importantly, once here, you are very much off the tourist track and into the real Mexico. In reality, the Mexico we experienced when we got to Mérida was a little too real (I thought of fleeing; Ian thought of de-fleaing), but if you stay at a five-star property, you should be just fine. The city is putting a lot of energy into pleasing gringos and more and more facilities are popping up.

For more information about Mérida, call ☎ 800/ 580-5547 in the U.S.

Shopping Mérida

In terms of actual shopping, I found Mérida heart-breaking. The *huipiles* (embroidered blouses worn by local women), for which the area is well known, were machine-made and not of the quality I remembered from years ago.

I wanted to buy Ian a *guayabera*—the local short-sleeved shirt worn by men in order to cope with the heat—but I couldn't find one that wasn't made with polyester. Prices for the poly blends were about $15, but because polyester makes you sweat, I passed on one. The few linen shirts I looked at cost $35 and were scratchy, poorly made, and not what I wanted. I paid $50 for a linen shirt at The Gap at my local mall, and it offered far better value.

While the market has a little of everything, I wish I could say I was knocked out by the local crafts and the straw items that are considered the best regional buy. Everything from hats and hammocks to place mats and little fans is available at low prices, but there is no charm here.

We took a *caleca,* or a local horse and buggy, right to the market and through the real people shopping zones of Mérida, and I wish I could tell you that this was magical. Unfortunately, Mérida is less than the poor man's Oaxaca.

Near the *zócalo,* Calles 58, 60, and 62 are considered the big shopping streets and are home to most of the branch stores, but it is the public market on the corner of Calle 57 and 67 that is the draw to tourists and locals alike.

Finds

CASA DE MONEDAS
Calle 63 no. 498, between Calle 60 and 58.

If I hadn't stumbled onto this antique shop and found the most wonderful pair of matched, hand-carved, antique virgins, I would have thought the trip to Mérida a wash in the shopping department. This shop is filled with all kinds of jumble and many religious items but no *retablos* (votive offerings).

Best Bets in Mérida

CALECAS

By far, the most fun we had in Mérida was driving around town in a *caleca.* We rode everywhere in one—did our shopping and shooting and sightseeing. We did have a few bait-and-switch problems with one of our owners, but on the whole, we adored the *calecas* and won't let you go to Mérida without committing yourself to at least one ride. (About $12 for a half hour.)

LEBANESE FOOD

Dinner at **Alberto's Continental** (Calle 64 and 57) was truly sensational. It was also fun to eat Lebanese food for a change. Full dinners for the two of us, with drinks and lots of wine, came to about $50. The restaurant is charming and rustic, but they also have a cute shop that they said they plan to close. Sorry. Ian bought a parrot for his kitchen in Suffolk for $25. He overpaid.

SIZE CONVERSION CHART

· ·

WOMEN'S DRESSES, COATS AND SKIRTS

American	3	5	7	9	11	12	13	14	15	16	18
Continental	36	38	38	40	40	42	42	44	44	46	48
British	8	10	11	12	13	14	15	16	17	18	20

WOMEN'S BLOUSES AND SWEATERS

American	10	12	14	16	18	20
Continental	38	40	42	44	46	48
British	32	34	36	38	40	42

WOMEN'S SHOES

American	5	6	7	8	9	10
Continental	36	37	38	39	40	41
British	$3^1/_2$	$4^1/_2$	$5^1/_2$	$6^1/_2$	$7^1/_2$	$8^1/_2$

CHILDREN'S CLOTHING

American	3	4	5	6	6X
Continental	98	104	110	116	122
British	18	20	22	24	26

CHILDREN'S SHOES

American	8	9	10	11	12	13	1	2	3
Continental	24	25	27	28	29	30	32	33	34
British	7	8	9	10	11	12	13	1	2

MEN'S SUITS

American	34	36	38	40	42	44	46	48
Continental	44	46	48	50	52	54	56	58
British	34	36	38	40	42	44	46	48

MEN'S SHIRTS

American	$14^1/_2$	15	$15^1/_2$	16	$16^1/_2$	17	$17^1/_2$	18
Continental	37	38	39	41	42	43	44	45
British	$14^1/_2$	15	$15^1/_2$	16	$16^1/_2$	17	$17^1/_2$	18

MEN'S SHOES

American	7	8	9	10	11	12	13
Continental	39½	41	42	43	44½	46	47
British	6	7	8	9	10	11	12

INDEX

ABOUT THE AUTHOR

Suzy Gershman is an author and a journalist who has worked in the fiber and fashion industry since 1969 in both New York and Los Angeles, and has held editorial positions at *California Apparel News, Mademoiselle, Gentleman's Quarterly,* and *People* magazine, where she was West Coast Style editor. She writes regularly for various magazines and her new essays on retailing are text for Harvard Business School. She frequently appears on network and local television; she is a contributing editor to *Travel Holiday.*

Mrs. Gershman lives in Connecticut with her husband, author Michael Gershman, and their son, Aaron. Michael Gershman also contributes to the *Born to Shop* pages.

Want to Go Shopping with Suzy Gershman?

What does Suzy Gershman do on vacation? She goes shopping, of course. But she takes people with her. If you've ever dreamed about shopping with the world's most famous shopper, this could be your chance.

Several times a year, **Born to Shop Tours** venture forth to Suzy's favorite destinations when she takes time to really show off her best finds. The pace is busy but relaxed compared to her regular schedule; several trips are booked through cruise lines to maximize the relaxation possibilities and to cut down on the stresses of transportation and dealing with luggage . . . but you do have to carry your own shopping bags.

Excursions often include lunch at just the right charming spot (perfect for resting tired feet), trips into back rooms and private warehouses not often seen by the public, or opportunities to buy at special discounted rates reserved just for Suzy's guests.

While the schedule varies from year to year, there's almost always a trip to New York and a Mediterranean cruise or two. Space is limited to ensure the intimacy of the group and experience. To find out about current plans or to inquire about arranging your own tour, call Giants at ☎ 800/442-6871; ask for Bonnie.

Frommer's Born to Shop guides are available from your favorite bookstore or directly from Macmillan Publishing USA. For credit card orders, call ☎ 1-800- 428-5331 (AMEX, MC and VISA).

Name _____

Address _____ Phone _____

City _____ State _____

Please send me the following **Frommer's Born to Shop** guides:

Quantity	Title	Price
_____	Born to Shop Caribbean Ports of Call	$14.95
_____	Born to Shop France	$14.95
_____	Born to Shop Great Britain	$14.95
_____	Born to Shop Hong Kong	$14.95
_____	Born to Shop Italy	$14.95
_____	Born to Shop London	$14.95
_____	Born to Shop Mexico	$14.95
_____	Born to Shop New England	$14.95
_____	Born to Shop New York	$14.95
_____	Born to Shop Paris	$14.95

Total for **Frommer's Born to Shop** Guides $ _____
Please include applicable sales tax

Add $3.00 for first book's S & H, $1.00 per additional book:
$ _____

Total payment: $ _____

Check or Money Order enclosed. Offer valid in the United States only. Please make payable to Macmillan Publishing USA.

Send orders to:
Macmillan Publishing USA
201 West 103rd Street
Attn: Order Department
Indianapolis, IN 46290

BS97